FAREHAM D-DAY 50 YRS ON

A COMMUNITY REMEMBERS

 **FAREHAM** BOROUGH COUNCIL

CIVIC OFFICES   CIVIC WAY   FAREHAM   HAMPSHIRE

A COMMUNITY REMEMBERS

Compiled & Edited
by
Kate Thompson
on behalf of
Fareham Borough Council

PUBLISHER'S NOTE
The Publishers accept no responsibility for the accuracy of personal accounts printed in this book. All accounts have been transcribed and published from interviews with members of the public, as shown under the acknowledgements section of this book.

Compiled and Edited by Kate Thompson
Book Design by Ray Pearce
Project Co-ordinated by Bob Leach

Published by
Fareham Borough Council
Civic Offices, Civic Way, Fareham
Hampshire PO16 7PP

All rights reserved. No part of this book may be reproduced, stored in a retrieval system or transmitted in any form, without the prior permission of the publishers.

ISBN 0 - 9523127 - 0 - 0

Typeset by PDQ Printing, in Palatino Light
Printed by PrintArea, Fareham

© 1994 FAREHAM BOROUGH COUNCIL

CONTENTS

FOREWORD
7

INTRODUCTION
9

ONE
FAREHAM'S ROLE
13

TWO
DRAMATIC EVENTS
23

THREE
THE PROFESSIONALS
35

FOUR
HOMELIFE
53

FIVE
WARTIME WORKERS
71

SIX
CHILDHOOD MEMORIES
93

ACKNOWLEDGEMENTS
119

FOREWORD

How often have you heard people say 'I wish I had recorded the stories of my friends and relatives.' It is a regret that many of us feel but all too often it is something which is voiced when it is too late. Those memories of our friends, parents and grandparents, of events far removed from our own today, are fascinating and highly entertaining. But sadly they are often lost.

This is becoming true of the memories of the Second World War. There have been many books written about the war but it is only through the first hand accounts of ordinary people, that we can get a clear picture of what every day life was like at that time.

With this in mind, Fareham Borough Council decided to embark on an oral history project to gather together memories from local people and compile a record of what life was like 'on the home front' during the war years leading up to D-Day in June 1944.

Fareham played an important role in the preparations for that fateful day and this book chronicles many local events that preceded it. This book shows that Fareham people had to endure their fair share of hardships but that their resolve never weakened.

The Borough Council is very proud to present their stories. They represent the deeply-felt reminiscences of a generation who lived through one of the greatest upheavals of all time and certainly in the whole of our nation's history. They are a fine way of helping to commemorate the 50th anniversary of the D-Day landings. I commend them to you.

Councillor Dr H G Jerrard
Chairman Policy and Resources Committee
Fareham Borough Council
April 1994.

INTRODUCTION

This is the story that until now has remained untold. It is the account of how ordinary Fareham people were affected by an extraordinary event in our nation's history. Much has already been written about D-day itself and the importance of what was to become the greatest military operation by allied forces – an operation which changed the course of the war in Europe. Little, however, has been said about the crucial role Fareham played in the events of D-Day and how the build-up to this operation changed the borough and its people.

With that in mind, Fareham Borough Council wanted to record for future generations the personal war memories of people living in the area during the early 1940's. The Council decided it should be an oral-history project, so that anyone with memories of that time could contribute to the story. In addition to gathering taped recordings, which will be held as archive material for future generations, this book was compiled so that the story of Fareham's D-Day memories would be readily available for all to enjoy. Volunteers were drafted in to visit local people and record their memories. They were trained in interviewing techniques by Donald Hyslop, an expert in oral history. Over cups of tea and on some lucky occasions, fondant fancies, our interviewers recorded the vivid details of wartime memories in the comfort of the contributors' living rooms.

It was important from the outset that this project should be a living account of what life was like during the early 1940's. Every detail, no matter how trivial, was recorded in order to give a true picture of life in Fareham during the war years and in particular those important months leading up to June 6 1944. The aim of an oral history project is to capture not only the hard facts but the emotion felt by ordinary people. By the very nature of oral history, you are relying on memories that however vivid, may not recall precise dates and data. However, these memories are valid because they capture a mood through individual recollections of an event or experience.

What perhaps makes this project unique is that in addition to the volunteer interviewers, the Council employed the services of a trained journalist, whose brief was to search out the more unusual aspects of community life – and to find some of the people in this book, who under normal circumstances would have been unable to contribute because they had moved out of the area.

The famous British reserve often means that good stories remain untold to a wider audience because the people concerned are too modest to come forward or feel their story is not of sufficient importance.

All too often it is these 'modest' people who provide the greatest insight into what life was really like and how people felt during those difficult days. Their stories may not be heroic or sensational but nevertheless they played their part – and for this reason it is important to record their story for future generations.

Many books have been written and will continue to be written about the Second World War and in particular the military side of the D-Day operation. But this book, although concentrating on the period leading up to the events of June 6 1944, provides a social history relating to life in Fareham during the war years.

It is the culmination of a ten month project, which combined with the many local exhibitions and work by schools and local groups, marks the 50th anniversary of D-Day.

When the anniversary is long gone, this collection of memories will provide a lasting record of what it was like to live in Fareham at that dramatic time.

EDITOR'S NOTE

On a personal note, I feel honoured to have been given the opportunity to compile and write this book.

The months of research and interviewing have been fascinating and my only hope is that I have been able to retell these personal accounts in an informative and interesting way.

I have thoroughly enjoyed listening to the tales of what life was like half a century ago. It never ceases to amaze me how people lived through such a difficult period of uncertainty and fear, whilst still retaining their sense of humour.

After hearing how many people coped with the hardships and restrictions of every day life and the long working hours they endured, I truly believe that we owe them a great debt of gratitude.

To everyone who contributed to this book – thank you.

KATE THOMPSON.

ONE

June 6 1944 holds a special place in the hearts of Fareham people – for this was the day when the course of the war was set to change. In the previous months, they had witnessed a massive military build-up, befriended the troops who had arrived in such vast numbers and anticipated what was surely to follow.....this was their D-Day.

After many weeks of waiting and wondering, the day had finally arrived when all their questions were to be answered. Many locals had a sneaking suspicion that the invasion was imminent. After all, why else would this quiet market town and its surrounding community have been literally swamped by troops from the Combined Allied Expeditionary Forces.

Up until then, Fareham had been party to one of the best kept secrets of the war and now they could all witness 'history in the making'; happy in the knowledge that they had done their bit to make the soldiers' last days before combat as comfortable as possible. The kindness shown by the Fareham people was to become an abiding memory for those servicemen stationed within the borough, in the run-up to D-Day.

A warming cup of tea brewed for the troops, from rations they could ill afford to share, was a simple gesture but one that was nevertheless greatly appreciated by the servicemen. The soldiers were welcomed into peoples' homes without questions needing to be asked. They were given hot water for baths and invited to share meals with Fareham families before settling down to a friendly game of cards.

It was as if the Fareham people knew what lay ahead for those brave young men. Most of all they wanted to show their gratitude there and then, while the soldiers were still in their midst.

Prior to D-Day the borough of Fareham had been a bit of a sleepy kind of place, where nothing much of any note ever happened. Certainly, Fareham had suffered its fair share of bomb damage but in comparison with its neighbours, Portsmouth and Southampton, the borough had escaped pretty lightly. Life ambled on, much the same as it had always done.

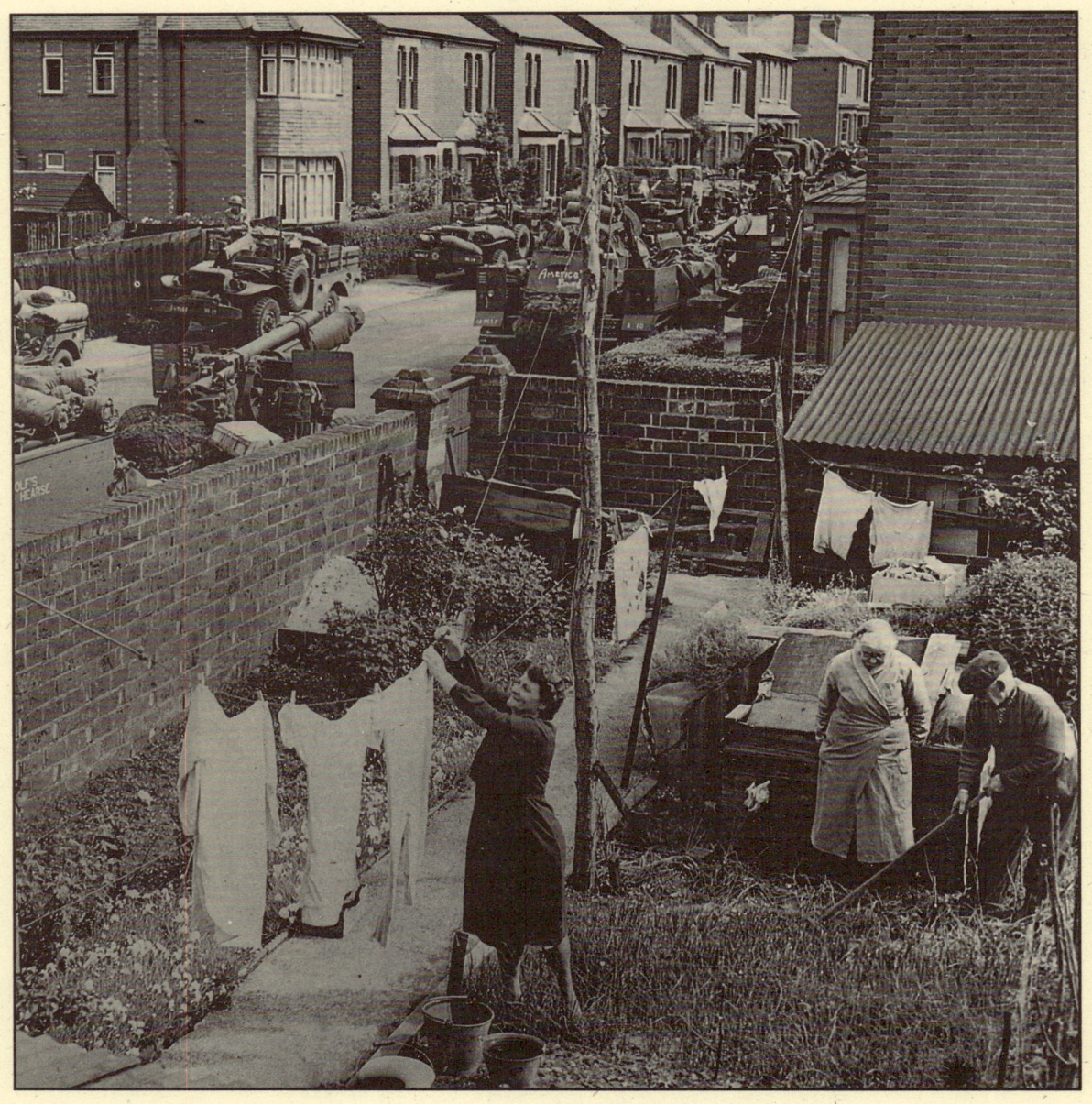

There were restrictions of course, with rationing on most essentials and few luxury items to be found, even if you had the money to pay for them.

By the time preparations for D-Day were underway, most people had had their fill of the war. They were tired of working so hard, they were tired of eating the same old food, they were tired of having to turn out night after night from the warmth of their beds to the damp of the Anderson shelter – they were just plain tired.

With the arrival of thousands of soldiers preparing for the Normandy campaign, Fareham and its people suddenly felt they were in the place that really mattered. They could see with their own eyes that something was going to happen in order to bring an end to the conflict – and the years of deprivation and hardship.

Their communities were plucked from obscurity and all of a sudden they were in the thick of it and they loved it. Places such as Sarisbury, Warsash, Locks Heath and Portchester were no longer just quiet little backwaters, they were of strategic importance to the war effort. Village greens were transformed from grassy play areas that had hitherto been the venue for annual fetes and carnivals, to canvas covered camps that became home to hundreds of troops.

Men slept in or under the tanks that lined the roadsides and seemed to work day in and day out preparing their vehicles. They water-proofed them to ensure the sea water did not damage them during the landings and made sure that all the mechanical parts were in A1 condition.

Fareham people could marvel at the sheer number of men involved in the forthcoming military operation. In many cases, they had the opportunity to meet people from the other side of the world for the first time ever. The Canadian and American troops were greatly admired for their good manners and they reminded the women of their Hollywood idols on the silver screen. It was a dramatic moment that has remained etched on the memories of all those who lived through it. Half a century on they can recall the names of the soldiers they met as if it were only yesterday.

To understand the impact of the D-Day preparations on the people of Fareham, it is vital to look at what life was like in the borough prior to the build-up to D-Day. Britain had

been at war for nearly five years and the toll on family life had been dramatic. Many loved ones had been lost but families were forced to get on with their lives as best they could.

Prior to the hostilities, Fareham had been a quiet but prosperous market town, whose main economy was based on farming, brickmaking and strawberry growing. Historically, it lived in the shadow of its neighbouring cities both of which were major ports. To the east was Portsmouth, an important naval base, to the west was Southampton, at that time the country's busiest commercial port. Between the wars, both cities developed and grew due to geographic and strategic factors, while Fareham remained a relatively small, close knit community largely unaffected by the growth of its neighbours.

It retained its market town character and altered little in appearance. The population was largely static during those years and families whose roots went back several generations were the backbone of the community. The same was true of the villages lying around Fareham. But war was to change the character of such places as Warsash, Titchfield and Sarisbury forever. Fareham could be excused for feeling like a 'piggy-in-the-middle' town. However it was the very nature of its location which was to make it of such strategic importance to the war effort.

From the outbreak of war in 1939, the Monday cattle market was still held and the town centre remained compact but accessible. As war progressed, however, there came about an ever increasing number of restrictions to daily life. In 1940, basic rationing was introduced, which imposed upon the general public limited availability in the supplies of such basic items as butter, sugar, ham and bacon. This was to be only the beginning of a long and difficult time for those living on the home front.

With the leadership of Winston Churchill from 1940 and the stern resolve of the Great British public, there was a mood within the country to sacrifice all creature comforts in an effort to support 'our boys.' Identity cards became a way of life, with proof in your pocket, the only way to travel through the borough. Hard work was accepted as necessary by those on the home front and work of national importance kept some men at home producing items for the war effort. But with so many of the country's traditional workforce away at war, it became necessary to draft in other hands to do the work.

The war brought about a dramatic social change for women. They entered the traditionally male workplace on production lines in factories and on the land. Until this time, all most women could expect was shop work or life in service with a local wealthy family before marriage and home life. But the war put an end to all that and opened up opportunities for women – the old order was to change forever...life would never be the same again.

At home, mothers became expert in making meagre rations go round and by testing their imagination to the limit – somehow they managed to produce appetising meals. Basic rationing by 1944 for an adult included; eight ounces of sugar, two and a half pints of milk, two and a half ounces of tea, four ounces of butter, two ounces of cheese, two ounces of margarine, four ounces of bacon, three ounces of beans and three ounces of sweets. Each person was allowed 31 eggs a year, so dried egg became an essential ingredient in the kitchen. The meat ration was one shilling's worth of carcass meat and two pence worth of canned meat. This could be supplemented by the occasional black market purchase and for special occasions, such as weddings, friends and family would often save up rations of dry

fruit and sugar over a number of weeks to make the wedding cake. Clothing was also rationed, with each person receiving 66 coupons a year. Children would find themselves wearing hand-me-downs from brothers, sisters or neighbours' youngsters. Hems were taken up and let down as needs be and mothers became expert in making clothing from all types of materials. Blankets were used to make warm, hard-wearing coats and often old curtains would be transformed into a suitable outfit.

Sewing and knitting were essential pastimes for women and local dressmakers were always busy with alterations. They made clothes as stylish as possible from lengths of material bought after many months of saving ration coupons. One of the first items that women had to make were the black-out curtains, which were soon to become a necessary feature of every window in the country. The sewing skills learnt in those days remain with many of the women who lived through the war years and some of those interviewed for this book still make all their own clothes.

Times were undoubtedly hard on the home front but as June 1944 approached, there was a general feeling within the country that something had to happen to bring hostilities to a head. As Fareham and the surrounding communities filled with tanks and vehicles ready for the invasion, all the locals knew that something was afoot – the only question was...when!

Even though people were busier than ever, working to a punishing schedule, they seemed to have more time for each other. Whenever you ask what life was like then, the overwhelming response is that it was friendlier and there was a real sense of community.

The thousands of troops who made their temporary home in Fareham and the borough communities, were warmly welcomed by the locals. Their doors were always open to the gallant young men – British, American and Canadians. Although people were thrown together, these chance meetings prompted great acts of kindness on both sides. Servicemen would share their rations and thrill the local children with gifts of chocolate and a chance to clamber over their tanks. For their part, the locals were pleased to share their rations with the young men – and their kindness must have boosted the troops' morale no end.

In the weeks leading up to the big-push, friendships blossomed and some Fareham families are still in contact with servicemen who found themselves on their doorsteps.

Although the troops were only in Fareham for a relatively short time, strong bonds were formed.

In the sophisticated '90's it is difficult to imagine the effect of this sudden influx of men from every corner of the globe. Many locals happily reveal that they were not well travelled. They stayed within their communities and trips to Portsmouth and Southampton were generally the farthest they would stray and rarely would they venture beyond.

Suddenly they were meeting people from far off lands who were willing to lay down their lives for the sake of freedom.

The home front, for the most part, had been inward looking – everyone playing their role and getting on with their lives, against a backdrop of world turmoil. However, with the arrival of thousands of troops, Fareham was drawn into the larger picture.

They were party to one of the greatest secrets of the conflict – and it was a confidence they were happy to keep.

In the coming chapters, Fareham people will tell in their own words how they lived their lives and the full effect that D-Day had on their families.

June 6 1944 holds a special place in the hearts of Fareham people – for this was the day when the course of the war was set to change. In the previous months, they had witnessed a massive military build-up, befriended the troops who had arrived in such vast numbers and anticipated what was surely to follow.....this was their D-Day – and this is their story.

———————— ◆ ————————

TWO

Thanks to its geographic situation and the fact it was not on the German's hit list for bombing raids, Fareham escaped mass devastation. While Portsmouth and Southampton were major targets, the Fareham area remained relatively unaffected by enemy bombardment. But there were occasions when it was not so lucky and local residents would find their world turned upside down.

There were undoubtedly many dramatic events which occurred during the build up to D-Day and there are people still living in the borough who can recall these chilling episodes. When a doodlebug landed in Park Gate, the small community suddenly found itself in the thick of it. It is believed that this was the first doodlebug or V1 to land in this country and certainly the people of Park Gate had never seen anything like it.

Nearly fifty years on, Roy Fay from Bursledon, has devoted a life time to finding out what happened on that fateful night, when 'all hell broke loose' on his street. Because an unknown weapon was involved, a security cordon was thrown around the area and the incident has been shrouded in mystery for years. However, Mr Fay has tirelessly worked to uncover the truth...and now his story can be told.

"It was May 30 1944 and the Canadians were due to move out at 5 o'clock in the morning. They were loaded up with mines and shells and when the doodlebug landed at 1.00 a.m. there was chaos."

Mr Fay was only 14 years old at the time but he can still remember the massive disruption which followed the attack.

"I had gone to bed and we heard the warning, then we heard this terrible noise. There was a massive explosion and all this ammunition, big and small, started to go up. We were in the shelter by then.

Not very long after we could hear all these vehicles starting up and driving away. They were moving blazing vehicles away from peoples' houses to a place of safety.

"The next day, from our garden wall we could see that there had been a high canvas screen erected around the tanks that were blown up. The RAF were there – they were connected with the crash and accident rescue team. For three days afterwards the residents had to get out because they were exploding shells from ten in the morning to 4 o'clock in the afternoon.

"Nobody had ever seen a flying bomb and this was the first one to land in this country. Three houses were completely destroyed and countless others were damaged.

"They lost two Sherman tanks, four self-propelled gun tanks, a jeep and three motorcycles. One of the motorcycle wheels went right through the roof of a bungalow 800 yards away. The troops used to sleep alongside the pavement and in gardens, so we couldn't

Bomb damage in Park Gate

work out how none of them were killed. But it turned out the Canadians were in a house having a farewell party, so they escaped undamaged.

"The whole area was completely packed with troops. Some had been there a month and others were in and out within a few days. They used to come in and ask if they could cook an egg. You didn't ask where they'd got the egg – that was their business.

"The women in the road would make tea for them, when they could and if there were plenty of apples about they would make them apple tarts. They were a friendly, smashing bunch of blokes. Girls could walk about through those troops and there would never be any problem at all."

Park Gate residents felt so grateful to the Canadian troops, who had acted so promptly to avert further disaster, that they wanted the world to know of their bravery.

"A petition was started, to have the Canadian troops recognised for their bravery. Locals went from house to house to collect signatures and eventually put the petition in the Post Office so people could sign it."

───────── ◆ ─────────

Eight troops received a citation for bravery for their actions on that night. The citation states that the soldiers removed or assisted in driving vehicles to a safe area and acted calmly and courageously in the most hazardous conditions.

One Canadian serviceman, Jim Morice, who was there on that night, has special memories of that doodlebug attack.

"I had just gone to bed in a shelter I had rigged along a wall. I heard a weird sound, then it cut out. I saw a flash just before it hit the SP about 50 yards from me. I knew it wasn't a regular bomb and later on after we had seen and heard a lot of V1's, I knew what it was. We were very lucky as only one of my drivers was wounded. Barney Leary was hospitalised but came back to us later on in the action. As we had no replacement for him I drove his SP in on D-Day.

"We were quite concerned about the people of Park Gate having their homes ruined and their lives disrupted but didn't get a chance to talk to them as we had such a short time to get replacements, serviced and water-proofed, ready to load onto landing craft. As for the commendations, there were a lot of boys that night that deserved to be recognised as much or more than we did.

"A little incident happened that night in Park Gate that might interest you. After we got all the vehicles away that we could and had taken them to safety down a side street, I headed down that way to get a head count for casualties, when I met a young lady running towards me when things were getting too hot for comfort. I grabbed her and she said: 'Are you a soldier?' I said I was, so she said: 'I have a shell in my bed.'

"We ran into her house, up the stairs and there was a 105mm projectile lying on the bed, scorching the blankets. The nose cone had blown, so it was safe enough, so I took a stick and rolled it onto the floor. Her father had gone into her room and sat on the bed when the shell came through the roof and it landed right beside them. It had come backwards through the air, I guess two or three hundred yards. They asked me if they could keep it, I told them it was of no use to us.

"But I heard that the 'Powers that Be' found out that they had a shell in the house and made everyone in the area evacuate until it could be taken away by the demolition people. I went by there after daylight, nobody was around but the projectile was standing in the middle of the street. I often think of the young lady and think that she was a very brave person, as were many of the local people that night."

―――――― ◆ ――――――

Another Canadian soldier, Allan Davis – a former medical orderly with the 13th Field Artillery – was on the scene that night.

"The medical group of the regiment, of which I was a part, were a few miles away from Park Gate when we got a call about the raid.

"We arrived at the scene when many vehicles were on fire. Some were driven out of the way. At the time we were sure that it was a direct hit by a bomb. It wasn't until later that I learnt that it was a V1. The most remarkable thing was that there were no serious injuries and all the damaged vehicles were replaced within 48 hours."

In the citation that followed Mr Davis's act of bravery, it noted that he 'advanced as far forward as possible until assured no casualties required attention. Not until directed by the battalion commander did he return to unit lines.' Now aged 84, Mr Davis can recall the incident vividly but he is modest about his own involvement.

"Why I got mentioned for that compared with what else I went through, I don't know."

Undoubtedly, it is the grateful people of Park Gate that Mr Davis can thank for the recognition he received.

Some of the best dramatic episodes in a person's life happen when you least expect them. Young Gordon Murphy was no exception and little did he realise the adventure which was to unfold after a routine shopping trip into Fareham. He had been to the Monday market with his father – known as Uncle Spud – and they were in Woolworths when the air raid warning went off.

The German Airman's boot

"It was about 11 o' clock in the morning. We came out of Woolworths by the side entrance. We drove out of Fareham and at the top of Titchfield Hill we stopped the car to see the raid starting over Portsmouth. We saw a German plane go in and climb quickly, I presume some anti-aircraft hit him as he came straight out over to Titchfield and when he got to the Stubbington area something dropped out of the plane and just after that one of the crew jumped out."

Gordon Murphy and his father watched where the man landed and with purpose in his voice, Uncle Spud declared: "Right, we'll go and pick this chap up." They turned into Ranvilles Lane and went along to find the airman hanging from an apple tree.

"He was surrounded by locals with pitchforks and nobody was going near him. My father got him down from the tree, put him in the car and took him to Fareham police station with his parachute.

"He couldn't speak English at all and he said nothing for the whole journey. I sat behind him and I can still remember the little bald patch on the back of his head and he was wearing a very nice gold watch. He didn't struggle or anything, he just went quietly. I should think he was quite a nice chap, he wasn't stroppy or anything like that."

At the police station, Uncle Spud demanded a receipt for the German officer and after some argument with the policeman on duty he was given one. Mr Murphy and his Dad returned to the farm to find out what else had fallen from the plane before the German officer jumped out...and there on the ground was the officer's sturdy, leather boot.

They did think about returning it to its rightful owner at the police station but thought better of it after all the fuss over the receipt.

The boot is a treasured reminder of that eventful day in the Murphy household and now it has its pride of place in the D-Day museum at Portsmouth.

———————— ◆ ————————

Mrs Diane Barnato-Walker had a bird's eye view on D-Day as the allied forces made their way across the Channel, for she was flying overhead on a mission to Gosport. For most of the war, Mrs Barnato-Walker was in the Air Transport Auxiliary based at Hamble – the first all-woman ferry pool in the country – and she can easily claim to have had one of the best views of Operation Overlord.

"The day before D-Day there was a tremendous gale and a lot of damage was done. They needed an Auster, which was an army spotter plane, flying to Gosport, so I took it there on D-Day itself – to replace one that had blown over the day before.

"It was still quite windy but as I flew all along the coast, past Fareham, I saw the build-up of the ships and the Bailey Bridges. The night before the tanks had rumbled past my cottage on the edge of the Hamble and I waved to them as they went by." The ATA was responsible for delivering planes safely to aerodromes throughout the length and breadth of the country. Mrs Barnato-Walker joined up with only 10 hours flying experience under her belt but the training she received made her capable of handling almost any wartime aircraft. "I had learnt to fly just before the war at Brooklands. England was desperately short of pilots and they put out a call for any civilian pilots. Initially they wanted them for taking messages but then it was decided they should deliver all the brand new aircraft to the squadrons which were based all over the country. Every single aeroplane flown by the RAF had been flown by an ATA pilot and at that time we didn't have radios and you had to find your way by map reading.

"I came in during 1941 and trained in light aircraft to start with. There were six different categories of aircraft that you could train to fly but I never did the four engines.

"A taxi programme was organised and sometimes you were the taxi pilot and sometimes the delivery pilot. This meant that if you were going from Hamble to, say, Eastleigh or Worthy Down, the taxi pilot would take you there and then off you went with your delivery. Sometimes the trip would be there and back and sometimes you would deliver two to three planes in a day. If you got stuck in a place because of bad weather, it was too bad, you just stayed there. It was frowned on if you tried to make your way back despite the weather because you had a date."

Many budding pilots would envy her proud boast that she flew 250 Spitfires or 'Spits' as she lovingly refers to them, in addition to many other types of aircraft.

"I enjoyed the Spitfires the most and they were the only aircraft that went right through the war. I flew 250 of them without breaking any.

"When you delivered the aeroplanes they were so pleased to get them that nobody made any comment that a women had flown it. Women were accepted and there was no back-biting.

"The only thing we weren't allowed to do was fly flying boats from the sea – but you were allowed to as long as you took off from the land. And I can tell you they were more like a boat in the air."

Naturally there were some hairy moments during her flying missions but Mrs Barnato-Walker, who is Commodore of the Association, can now make light of her experiences.

"I was shot at once in an Anson coming back over Reading. Jim Morrison, the famous record-breaking pilot who married Amy Johnson, was flying it and I was beside him. There were 13 or 14 people on board and you weren't supposed to have more than 10 or so. We were coming back towards a weather front which was lying north/south over Maidenhead and as we came towards Reading we saw plumes of smoke.

"They had steam trains there and I thought the smoke was from a train blowing off steam but as we flew towards the front, with the sun behind us, we suddenly saw a German plane and we could see the tracer coming from it. Jimmy Morrison pulled the plane right up and luckily he didn't hit us."

However, it was not just attacks from the enemy that ATA pilots had to avoid, there was also plenty of so called `friendly fire.'

"We used to get shot at by our own side, chiefly over the Bristol Channel. I used to take Hurricanes from Langley via Slough and as I flew across the Bristol Channel you would feel it because it used to bump the wings a bit – but you never thought anything of it."

———————◆———————

Stray bombs that missed their intended target often fell in the borough, flattening homes and bringing misery to countless families. One fateful night in April 1944, the Hayter family suffered terrible losses at the hands of the German bombers. Horace and Lily Hayter were in their Anderson shelter when their home at 102 The Crossway, Portchester, was bombed.

They did not realise what had happened until they came out of the shelter and found their chickens running amok. Gladys Andrews, the Hayter's niece, can remember how badly her family suffered that night.

"My sister-in-law, nephew and niece died when a bomb landed on their terrace. They had sheltered under the stairs rather than going to the shelter and were suffocated. The Hayters were a well known local family. My father and four uncles all worked for the family business, W Hayter and Sons in West Street."

Bomb damage in Colenso Road, Fareham

They were the local blacksmith, wheelwright, coachbuilders and undertakers. Their workshops were destroyed by the blast which killed Gladys' sister-in-law and children. The sad task of making their coffins had to be performed in the garden amid the rubble of their business premises.

◆

A bomb which fell on Colenso Road, Fareham at the start of the war changed Joyce Kingswell's life. She lost her home and for the rest of the war stayed with friends – coping with her life without the comfort of her husband at hand. Like many newly-weds, her world had been wrenched apart at the start of the conflict. Her husband saw active service throughout the war and she made the best of her life waiting for the moment when he would return.

"The bomb fell in September 1941, my husband was home on leave from the Air Force. It was a very quiet night, that night. The sirens had gone off at about 10.30 p.m. and then the all clear was sounded.

"At about 11 o'clock, suddenly the guns opened up. There was an awful noise and a terrific whistling sound. My husband pushed me under the table so we would be safe. When

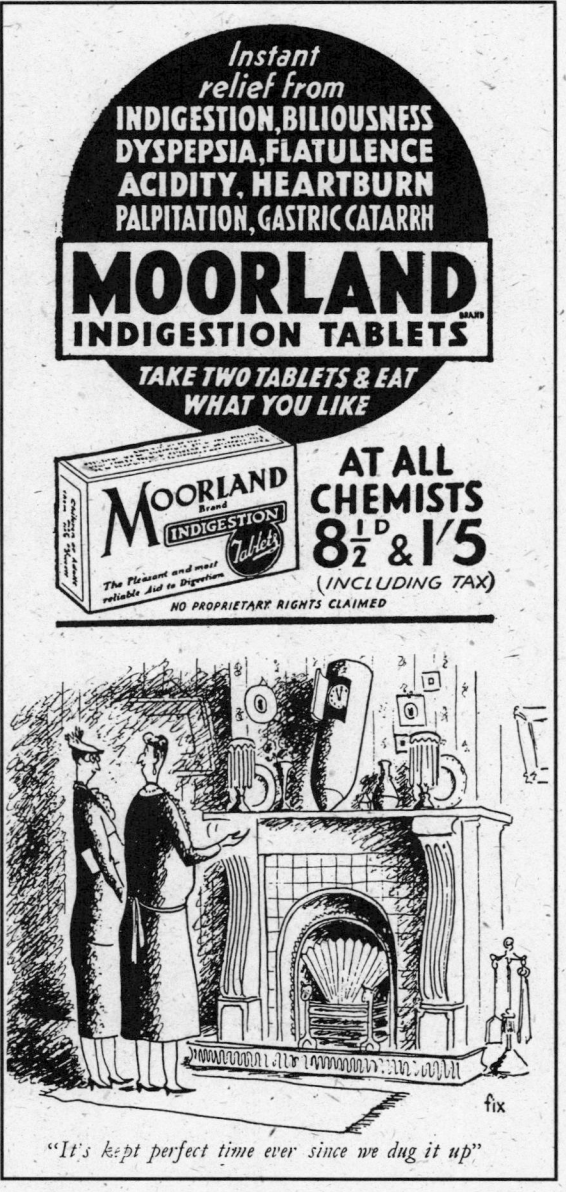

"It's kept perfect time ever since we dug it up"

it was all over I went to open the back door and there was just a wall of earth.

"And when I opened the door to the room we were sheltering in, the front door was leaning up against it. Upstairs there were lumps of earth as big as a settee on the bed. I thought it was fantastic that all that earth from the recreation ground should be thrown right over the roofs of our houses into our back gardens.

"If the bomb had hit the road instead of the recreation ground we would certainly have been killed because it was made from concrete. Nobody seemed to bother much about the destruction the bomb brought – they didn't make the fuss they make today."

Mrs Kingswell packed up what possessions she could, stored most of the larger objects and took the bare necessities with her when she moved in with a friend in Redlands Lane, Fareham. She worked in a Fareham grocers shop at a time when service was as important as the items which were sold. Service with a smile was expected and with no automatic tills, the shop assistants had to be adept at mental arithmetic – and of course, there was no decimalisation.

"I worked at Pinks, a big family grocers, at 90 West Street Fareham, opposite the old Post Office. It was a beautiful shop and they sold tip-top stuff. You could smell their coffee half way down West Street and there were drawers filled with different spices.

"In those days everything was weighed and we used to make deliveries. I can remember a boy being sent out to deliver a bar of soap that cost 2d. I can remember Oxo cubes cost a penny and you could get a big pot of jam for one shilling and four pence. We used to add up all the money ourselves. You had your own till and a float that you were responsible for."

Going to and from work, Mrs Kingswell saw the build-up of tanks on the streets of Fareham and can recall how the baby-faced Canadian servicemen seemed too young to be shaving let alone preparing for battle.

"There were tanks up Park Lane and all the surrounding roads. Every day they used to move these big tanks up and down. They were mostly Canadians and they were only boys. Just before D-Day there was an unending stream of tanks, hundreds and hundreds of them all making their way to Stokes Bay."

THREE

In any major conflict, it is important to have professionals who can be relied upon to maintain essential services and help day to day life run as smoothly as possible. Fareham was no exception to this rule and during the war years, these mostly unsung heroes played an important role in maintaining the status quo, such as it was.

It was vital to keep areas such as Fareham running as smoothly as possible from a practical as well as a morale boosting point of view. Times were hard enough, so it was imperative to have as many day to day services in operation. Imagine the chaos that would have prevailed, if the railway had not remained in operation, if the roads had not been cleared of bomb debris and if the banks had not continued to open for business.

Basic services that we often take for granted now, were indispensable during the war years. At the forefront of ensuring everything ran as near to normal as possible, was Fareham Urban District Council. As well as day to day duties, such as providing housing and playing fields for youngsters; emptying rubbish bins and setting the 1944 general rate – at five shillings and four pence in the pound, the Council took on new responsibilities and these were dealt with in the time honoured local government fashion.

There were committees for everything and much of the councillors' time during 1944 was seemingly taken up with reports, from the likes of the Billeting Officer, the Fire Guard Officer and the Local Air Raid Precautions Officer. But it was such attention to detail which was to help the Council maintain a grasp of what was going on in the local communities. Research into the Council's minute books of 1944 reveals, that a meeting of the Isolation Hospital Committee took place, to agree the appointment of a new nurse. It was decided to take on Mrs M.A.M Parfitt at a weekly wage of £2 15s. per week – less one shilling for every midday meal provided.

Other minutes show that in March 1944, the Roads and Works Committee reported that it was very difficult to buy dustbins and therefore decided that an application should be made to the Ministry of Supply, for the necessary permission to purchase five dozen dustbins.

The blackout was a serious matter during the war and there were penalties to be paid by those who did not adhere to the rules. At the Civil Defence Committee meeting of April 27 1944, the clerk reported that proceedings had been taken by the Police, in connection with the blackout at the British Restaurant in Osborn Road, Fareham, and a fine of £1 was imposed on the person in charge. But the kind hearted Council decided to pick up the bill for the fine as the restaurant manageress was absent due to illness at the time of the offence. Such was the ability of the Council to show a capacity for understanding, despite the pressures of administration during a state of war.

On the same date, it was reported that the number of billeted evacuees, including unaccompanied children, was 178 and the total number of people in requisitioned houses was 181. However, it appears there was the odd accident with these 'house guests' as the report detailed that two claims for damage to bedding by war-workers were received by the Council.

The day before D-Day, the Council was pre-occupied with the serious business of buying two ladders at a cost of £12 2s.6d. – but then life had to go on.

Mrs Rita Briggs, was a member of the Engineer's Department in Westbury Manor and a volunteer in the Fareham Council Control Room, which was set up to deal with emergencies in the borough.

"At the back of Westbury Manor, there were some purpose built shelters where we had to sleep when we were on duty all night and there was nothing much going on. There was condensation running down the walls and the blankets were more wet than dry. We would be woken up if something had happened and you would run to the Control Room and stay there for the rest of the night and then you were expected to go straight to work from there. This happened every other night for about two years.

"When there was a double red, that meant that the raiders were coming over in our direction and you had to contact people and tell them what was happening. We would contact the Police, the Fire people and Ambulance Service – there was a nucleus of people we would contact. Then when the all-clear came through from headquarters everyone would stand down and we would have a cup of tea. There were about a dozen of us on each shift.

The Controller was Mr Coward and there was a Deputy Controller and telephonists. During the night the Police would come in to see what was going on."

From the onset of war, the make-up of the Council's workforce had changed dramatically as all the young men had been called up to serve their country.

"When the war started, all the men went and in my department we were all women apart from the boss himself and one other man who had quite a hard time! The Treasurer's Department was on the ground floor at Westbury Manor, we were on the first floor and above us was the Medical Officer of Health – it wasn't such a big organisation in those days but it was very matey.

"We were responsible for highways, refuse collection, sewage disposal and recreation grounds. And if there was bomb damage and the road was blocked we had to clear it. It was elderly men who did that sort of thing because all the young men had been called up."

Rita Briggs (far right) with her Council colleagues

Nobody thought to ask for more money for the extra hours they were working and Mrs Briggs can remember that people took the extra jobs in their stride and just enjoyed being involved.

"When I went to the Council, I thought I was doing very well because I was earning £60 a year. I started in 1936 and I was there for 40 years. We didn't get paid anything extra for working in the Control Room but people didn't complain because it was exciting and there wasn't much else going on to be excited about.

"I don't think people were as emotional about these things as they are today. We took it as something that had to be done. The troops had work to do and so did we – we all worked together and I don't think we ever thought about the rights and wrongs and whether we were going to get paid or not. It never occurred to us."

Even though she was working all those hours, Mrs Briggs still found time to enjoy herself. There were always plenty of dances and lots of young servicemen looking for a dancing partner.

"There were always the troops about who wanted the girls to go to the dances, so we did enjoy ourselves. I was at the right age. We organised dances in Westbury Manor and then we got invited to the dances organised by the servicemen. They would come and pick us up in their lorries and they dropped us back afterwards. It was all pretty innocent and nobody got into any trouble. We were just trying to forget about the war."

It was a time of innocent good fun and the women of Fareham seemed to have little to fear. They were happy to invite the troops into their homes and 'while away' the hours, chatting about their respective families. The Canadian servicemen in particular made a great impression on the people of Fareham – however fleeting the friendships.

"The Canadians were lovely chaps. I went out with a woman who was staying with her husband at our house and we met some Canadians, who asked if they could come to our house and have a cup of tea. I said I wasn't sure because of my mother but they said they would bring some rations with them. So we went with them and they had one of those big, high vehicles that were called `Gin Palaces' for some reason and we climbed in the back. They told us we were going into one of the protected areas and we mustn't let on that we were there. So we got under the seats and they covered us up with rugs and off we went.

"We laid low going through the gates as we went past the sentry and we had to keep quiet while they went to get the stuff – it was a real adventure. When they came back, we drove home and I went to warn my mother and explained they were very nice chaps. They stood behind me and threw in their caps and said `Hello Ma'am' and everything was alright then. They had brought a tin of chicken, some butter and two or three other things. They sat down and had a meal in our house which we all enjoyed. They talked about their families and children back home, while we sat there eating our bread and their chicken. It's sad really because after that evening – we never saw them again."

───────────── ◆ ─────────────

Mrs Patricia Macdonald, from Portchester, began work with the Council straight from school, issuing identity cards in the Food Office at Forresters Hall and served from 1941 to 1946. She can remember being interviewed for her job at Westbury Manor by Mr Rands, who later became the Clerk to the Council.

"I had gone there just for the issue of ration books and I was singled out to be asked if I wanted to go onto National Registration and issue identity cards. I started as a temporary and eventually became a permanent member of staff. The identity cards were put out by the Council, although this duty was eventually taken over by the Food Office which was responsible for ration books. "At Forresters Hall, there was the `baby section' where they issued the concentrated orange juice and cod liver oil. It was such a dirty place, they had miles of documents going back years and they were all covered in dust – and this was still in the office where we were all working.

"The ration books were sent out annually and that involved a lot of overtime. To set up the identity card scheme, I believe they did a sort of census. Everybody was put on this list and they were issued with an identity number and depending on which area you were living in, you were given a different number and different letters in front of the number. There was an adult identity card which was blue, a buff coloured one for children under 16 and a yellow one for aliens. The C.I.D. in Fareham used to come to me when they couldn't trace the Irish labourers and I was able to tell them where they had moved to.

"I started at the big sum of £3 a week which was pretty good in those days, rising to five pounds a week."

Mrs Macdonald, was a great film buff but little did she realise that she was to meet some of her idols from the silver screen, while working in Fareham.

"We had some very interesting people coming into the office. I just joined after Vivien Leigh had been in to register because she and Lawrence Olivier, who was in the Fleet Air Arm and Ralph Richardson and his wife Muriel Forbes, were living in Newtown Road in Warsash. I saw Ralph Richardson at the bus station one afternoon in his uniform and he came into the office one day as well.

"I was an absolute film fan and I used to get film magazines and lap it all up. It was very nice to have two cinemas in Fareham, so if we were working late one night and we thought... `Oh we've had enough, let's go to the flicks' – it would help us to relax. We would watch the news reels and sometimes there were as many as three feature films a week, so you could go three times a week if you wanted to and sit in the `one and nines.'

"One of my favourite films was `Laura' starring Gene Tierney and I was mad for Fred Astaire and Ginger Rogers. I lapped up all the Alexander Korda films, they were so good and of course there were the English comedies. And I absolutely adored Trevor Howard. I remember once or twice I got a free ticket at the Savoy – films and books were all I was interested in.

"At lunchtime, I used to take my sandwiches into the `old rec' in Park Lane and take my Jane Austen to read – I read her all through the war because she was so relaxing."

Mrs Macdonald cycled everywhere during the war and the money she saved on her bus fares, was to help fulfil her dream of going to art college when the conflict was over.

"Going to work every day you would be in a military convoy. I used to cycle on the footpath and they would all be hanging out of the back of the lorries and pretend to pull me along. My cycle rides to the Food Office meant I was able to save the money which would have gone on fares and put it in the Post Office for when I went to college after the war."

Mrs Macdonald, had always had quite a flair for drawing and she put her artistic talent to good use, when she completed a sketch of General Montgomery. She sent him the portrait at the time of D-Day and was delighted to receive an acknowledgement from his office.

"I sketched the picture of General Montgomery the week of D-Day. I can remember while I was sketching seeing the planes going over to France, towing the gliders.

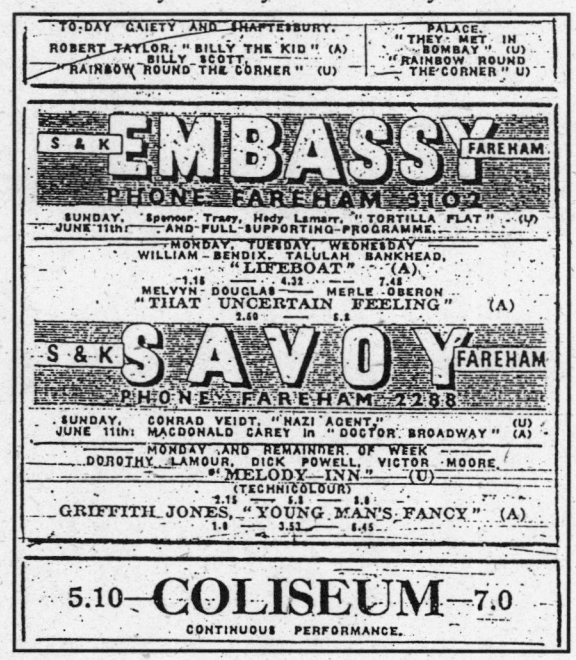

My parents came back from Portchester Castle and my father said something big was going to happen. I took Montgomery's likeness from a photograph, which was on the cover of the Illustrated Magazine and I sent him the portrait. And with all the excitement going on with D-Day, I couldn't believe that I received a letter of thanks from his ADC.

"I lived on the main road, leading up to Southwick where General Montgomery and Eisenhower were but it was very hush-hush and we didn't realise how close we were to everything. So the fact that he might have gone by in his staff car while I was sketching him seemed incredible to me."

───────────── ◆ ─────────────

Mr Harold Holdaway, was proud to serve with the local fire crew and for the most part he enjoyed his work. A practical man, he believed in getting on with the job in hand and making the best use of his time. But his attitude did not win him friends in all quarters. Fifty years on, he can still chuckle at the reactions of his superiors to some of his antics. They preferred to do everything by the book and found Mr Holdaway's methods slightly unorthodox. "Our family was attached to the local Volunteer Fire Service. My father did 34 years' service and was second officer. When the threat of war was imminent, I joined the Auxiliary Fire Service. Our family's knowledge of the fire service was very useful.

"I can still remember the procedure before the sirens were fitted. My wife Phylis and I lived in Beaconsfield Road and my father was in Gosport Road. When there was an alert, I would phone my father and he would come over to me and we would go together to the station which was two or three hundred yards away. As soon as the alarm went, I just left my bed and went off to do whatever I could. You were on call even after you had been on duty at the station all day.

"I got involved with all sorts of criticisms for the way I did things. For example, when the sirens were first installed in the station I got into trouble. The fire station was responsible for fitting the sirens and there was a fall of snow which clogged the sirens and they froze. When I came in that morning, I realised that none of these sirens would function, so I got a fire crew with a ladder and sent them round and told them how to free the sirens of snow.

"I was called up in front of the Chief Fire Officer. The Chief of Civil Defence who was responsible for the sirens had been in to see him and he was very annoyed at what I had done – but I thought it was better to get on and unclog the sirens as soon as possible.

"On another occasion, the Germans had been over and dropped a series of fire bombs down through West Street. I was with a fire crew at Boots the Chemist. At that time they used to run a private library and a fire bomb had landed in there. The door was locked and the fire was getting hold in there. So I broke down the plate glass door with an axe. There was a bit of criticism for that because they said I should have waited for orders."

Mr Holdaway may not have seen active service during the war years but he fought his own personal battle against petty red tape and bureaucracy. His candid recollections of the

Firemen on parade in Fareham Town Centre

frustration he felt at being given the wrong orders from on high and waiting weeks for supplies that never came, are both refreshing and revealing. He for one does not recall his fire service days, with the rosy hue that can often colour memories as the years pass by.

"It has always amazed me that we won the war at all. If the other side were worse than we were, they must have been pretty bad. There was so much bureaucracy and paperwork – it used to frustrate me.

"I'll never forget the day a notice was sent out from the Home Office that all fire extinguishers had to be tested to a certain pressure to make sure they were sound. A man was sent off with the necessary equipment to do this job. He came to me half way through the morning and told me that none of the extinguishers were standing up to the pressure and they were bursting. He showed me his orders and I realised they contained the wrong figures, so I told him he must stop at once – otherwise he would have gone round to all the stations and each extinguisher would have exploded.

"As the war went on I moved to Portsmouth, to the area workshops for the fire brigade. The mechanics at the workshop used to come to me when they were short of simple tools like files, hammers and spanners. We had to put an order in with the Ministry of Works, to say we wanted some tools. They came on lease/lend from America. Instead of lending us money, they sent materials and we paid for them after the war.

"Weeks went by and they didn't turn up. Suddenly a huge box arrived but there wasn't a spanner, nor a file or hammer to be seen. Instead the box contained the most intricate measuring instruments. The value of them must have been ten or twenty times more than the ordinary tools we were wanting.

"We had fire boats which were sent over lease/lend. They had American engines with a peculiar type of ignition system. One of them broke down and I found that it was the rotor arm that was causing the problem. We had no spares, so eventually I went to the Dockyard to see if they could help but they said they had none available. So I set to and made one. It was a crude job but it got the engine going. No sooner had I done it, than my senior officer came in with a box of rotors from the dockyard...It was a very frustrating time!"

This is the Gin
Gordon's
Stands Supreme
Start taking
PHYLLOSAN
to revitalize your Blood, improve your Circulation, strengthen your Nerves, increase your Stamina and Energy
PRE-UTILITY FURNITURE
SECOND HAND FURNITURE
82, HIGH ST.
JOCKEY POOLS
ZETTERS POOLS LTD
390-392 EUSTON ROAD, LONDON, N.W.1
Estd. 1933
14 Matches
3 Dividends, 50% 30% 20%
CAMP COFFEE
Don't blame your grocer if you have to 'WAIT FOR IT'
GOOD COFFEE CONCENTRATED
WILLS's CAPSTAN CIGARETTES
St. Margaret
Twice guaranteed
Standing behind the name St. Margaret are many years of experience in making Hosiery and Underwear. Link that experience with wartime Utility standard, and you get a double guarantee of value. Money—and coupons—are wisely spent on Utility Hosiery and Underwear bearing the St. Margaret name. Be sure to look for both marks when you buy St. Margaret.
Still the Best!
BIRD'S CUSTARD
"Got any More WASTE PAPER for Salvage?"
When you buy Parker Quink — buy CONCENTRATE too!
SHAVEX
NO SOAP—NO BRUSH—NO LATHER
IS USED BY BRITISH FORCES
Take no Imitations.
NEVER put your Salvage in the dustbin!

FINE, THANKS!
I eat something crisp and crunchy every day. When I can get it, I prefer
RYVITA
CRISP, NOURISHING DAILY BREAD
Barker & Dobson
CHOCOLATES
Barker & Dobson, famous confectionery
Smart, Health
Not when she has her own cake of
Gibbs
DENTIFRICE
GIVE YOUR TEETH A SHINE WITH GIBBS
To end all SKIN AILMENTS apply Germolene
Note these Facts
HEADACHE has one thing in common with Rheumatism, Neuritis, Toothache, Sleeplessness, Colds and 'Flu:
ZIXT
HAND SOAP
Makes hands clean — leaves them smooth
Berkertex
DESIGNED BY NORMAN HARTNELL
Cool candy stripes — perfectly styled. This delightful model is also available in charmingly patterned rayon.
HIP SIZES 36' — 42'
45'9
- 7 COUPONS
LEG TROUBLE, CUTS, PIMPLES, INFLAMMATION, BURNS, RASHES, INSECT BITES, ETC.
use
Germolene
— it soothes at a touch and heals your skin clean!
Why not be FIT and SLIM for Summer
By Regularly Taking
BILE BEANS
The Original Blood Purifying Medicine for BLOOD and SKIN COMPLAINTS
CLARKES BLOOD MIXTURE
At all Chemists & Stores.
DO YOU HAVE TO REMIND HER TO CLEAN HER TEETH ...?
Brilliant HEAD SQUARES.
Light-weight WOOL SQUARES.
HANDLEYS

Mr Ken Riley, from Fareham, joined the Special Constabulary with a group of local friends in 1938. He was a Chartered Accountant and when the war came, this was classified as a reserved occupation. As the conflict progressed, he was drawn into war reserve duties for the Police and found himself pounding the beat at £4 a week – taking the place of serving policemen who had been called up.

He managed to combine his Police duties, with running his accountancy firm throughout the war. He can recall that he received call up papers for the RAF and when he presented these to his superiors, he was asked what he would like to do. He stated that he would prefer to stay in the Police and run his own business. To this day he does not know what happened to those call up papers...

Mr Riley's beat, which went out as far as Catisfield to the west, Hoads Hill, Wickham, to the north and out to Cornaway Lane, Portchester in the east, was covered either on foot or by bicycle. He was responsible for keeping law and order within the area and would also work at the control room in Westbury Manor. If he was on a night shift, Mr Riley would often find himself manning the police phone based at the Westbury Manor headquarters. As soon as news of a raid came through, he had to alert Fareham Police Station and depending on enemy activity, he often worked through the night – until the all clear was sounded.

"There was no crime as we know it today, I can't remember anything like muggings or petty thieving going on. I can remember there was a suicide but I can't recall any murders or anything like that."

The police were also responsible for enforcing the black-out and Mr Riley can remember he preferred a softly-softly approach with offenders.

"If you were on night duty and you saw a chink of light coming from someone's window you used your discretion. I used to knock on the door and show them that there was a light shining and normally that would be enough. But if they were blatant you had no alternative but to report them and they would end up going before the Courts.

"I can remember one occasion, when we had a notification that there was a German plane about, so we went to Portsdown Hill to have a look. There was another crew with us and they eventually captured this German pilot and brought him to the police station. I can remember he was a big tall chap, about six foot two. I suppose he was shot down after doing a raid on Portsmouth."

Work shifts would run from 6.00 a.m. to 2.00 p.m., then 2.00 p.m. to 10.00 p.m. and 10.00 p.m. to 6.00 a.m. Despite this tough work pattern, Mr Riley soon became used to fitting his accountancy work around his police duties.

"You could work weekends and swap with other people to leave you free on other days during the week – sometimes it seemed like we were working 24 hours a day."

———————— ◆ ————————

The Reverend Ted Royds-Jones, the former curate of St Peters and St Pauls Church in the High Street, Fareham, was kept very busy during the war years. As well as caring for the spiritual needs of his parishioners, Rev. Royds-Jones taught maths and science at Prices Grammar School in Fareham.

"When the war started there was a shortage of teachers, so I combined the two jobs," recalled the 95 year-old churchman.

Although Fareham escaped the massive destruction of its neighbours, it did have its fair share of bomb damage. Rev. Royds-Jones was writing his sermon one evening at the school when an explosion in an adjacent road rocked the building to its very foundations. Tons of clay, thrown into the air by the blast, cascaded onto the school roof and the Reverend had to scuttle under his desk to escape the deadly shards of flying glass from the shattered windows.

In the build-up to D-Day, military vehicles began to arrive in the town and their allocated spaces were marked out on the road in white paint. At that time, the soldiers were busy preparing their vehicles for the forthcoming operation. They were constantly maintaining and water-proofing the engines against the harsh sea water.

"Every single road was lined each side with vehicles – it was choc-a-bloc. The soldiers were busy water-proofing their vehicles. They used two lots of grease so their vehicles would be alright when they went into the sea."

———————— ◆ ————————

Mr Pat Hamblin, would be the envy of anyone who hankers for the days when 'real' trains puffed their way along our rail network. For during the war years, he was a fireman on the steam trains that travelled along the Meon Valley line.

"I ran a pull or push from Alton through to Gosport down the Meon Valley line. I was a fireman then, from 1943 onwards. My duties included getting the steam engines ready, keeping the steam up, the water level up and making sure there was enough coal – I was a general dogsbody.

"I was 20 years old and looking back now I liked my job, even though it was quite difficult. We worked in 24 week cycles, carting war materials around. There was an underground factory at Salisbury, where they used to make 10,000 lb bombs and we used to transport the bombs and charges for the Navy – that sort of thing.

"Everything went on the railways in those days. There was very little road haulage. Plymouth, Portsmouth and Southampton were the worst places, as you could quite often get caught in air raids. Along the Meon Valley line it was quite easy and almost event free. The gangers, who used to keep the track in order, used to hand us rabbits, cabbages and carrots as we went by.

"Occasionally we would get caught in air raids. It was difficult because we couldn't hear the sirens, so at signal boxes along the route a man used to wave a light to warn us. We used to black out as much as possible with tarpaulins. There wasn't a great deal of danger – even if we were hit, the stuff wasn't going to explode because it wasn't primed.

"The most dangerous thing we carried was high octane fuel for aircraft. We were particularly wary when we were carrying that stuff but other than that we never really worried about what we had the other side of the tender.

"It wasn't evident that D-Day was coming. There was just a long slow build-up. A lot of stuff was being moved around but not enough to give you an inkling that something was afoot.

"And even when we realised something was going to happen, nobody knew where or when it would happen."

———————— ◆ ————————

A love of the water stood Mrs Rhona Moody, in good stead during her stint at HMS Tormentor in Warsash. As a serving Wren, she was responsible for crewing the duty boats which plied their way back and forth from the naval base.

Speaking from her Warsash home, overlooking the River Hamble, Mrs Moody remembered with fondness her time in the forces.

She and her colleagues were in charge of moving supplies and personnel by boat up and down the river. They were adept at scrambling from one craft to the next and 'tying up' on buoys.

"I learnt more in the Wrens than I ever did at school. It was good fun but very hard work. When I got married my hands, were calloused and covered in bruises. But I was lucky because a couple of the girls lost their little fingers on the ropes."

The Rising Sun in Warsash was the local pub but as Rhona was brought up to be teetotal, she used to prefer a hot cup of cocoa to keep out the evening cold.

Although details of the D-Day campaign were top secret, it was quite obvious to her that something big was being planned. On the day before the allied forces left for France, Mrs Moody can remember the dramatic sight of boats and landing craft stretching as far as the eye could see.

"There were so many boats you felt you could have walked from one to the other. I had never seen so many before, they stretched towards Southampton and down as far as St Catherine's Point, on the Isle of Wight."

The craft left silently under cover of darkness and Mrs Moody can still recall waking on that fateful day to discover they had all gone.

"We hadn't heard a thing and it was such a surprise to find they had all gone. Afterwards, we were confined to barracks for about two to three weeks. Everyone had a feeling of emptiness, it was almost like a bereavement – you just could not believe that they had gone."

───────── ◆ ─────────

Miss Edith Strebor, worked for a bank throughout the war and eventually transferred to the Fareham branch. As a clerk, she was used to working long hours for no extra pay –

just to get the job done. Such hardship had run in her family. When her father died in 1911, her mother had single-handedly brought up her four children. She worked until she was 68 years old and had to wait a further two years to receive her pension of 10 shillings a week.

Miss Strebor combined some fire watch duties with her work at the bank but her first concern was the care of her aged mother.

"I left home at eight fifteen in the morning to get to work for eight thirty and it was nothing to leave at half past eight at night or later. We worked thousands of hours for nothing, we literally worked night and day. People don't realise what we went through so they could have such a good life now."

She has an abiding memory of the build-up to D-Day and more importantly, the lightening speed with which the clean up operation began.

"I do remember prior to D-Day, the prolonged noise of tanks and armoured vehicles passing through West Street. On going home, we were astonished to find the road was just like a ploughed field and we wondered how long we would have to wait for it to be re-surfaced.

"We need not have worried because the next morning, on entering the bank, the road had been repaired to its original state. It was unbelievable and I don't think you would get that happening in peace time."

Soon now!

after five years
with the Services
HEINZ
57
will be home with you again

Always ready to serve

Leading Wren Mrs Joyce Vare, was stationed at HMS Daedelus in the run-up to D-Day – and when the raw recruits arrived for their ten week training, it was Mrs Vare who would note down their measurements.

"I was always astonished by how much they had grown during the training. They left Daedelus with stature – they really had put on inches."

The build-up to D-Day was going on all around her. It was so obvious that something was going to happen but she was not privy to the date of the invasion. A colleague of Mrs Vare, with whom she had served at HMS Collingwood earlier in the war, was in hospital. As she cycled to visit her, Mrs Vare was amazed to see just how many armoured vehicles were crammed onto the country roads.

"It seemed like there was somebody hidden under every twig and leaf. It was just unbelievable. I was at Daedelus for D-Day and the sea was just full of every type of craft you could imagine. My boyfriend at the time was out on one of the forts but he was back for D-Day. I went to see him and I can remember sitting on a bank with him and watching all the craft set sail. He had a very strong pair of binoculars, so we could see all the tanks and lorries being chained on – it was just fascinating to watch."

───────────── ◆ ─────────────

FOUR

Homelife, took on an increasingly important role during the war years. While the world outside was such an uncertain place – there was a great feeling of security when the front door was closed to the outside world. Lifestyle, in those days, was by no means lavish and most people in the Fareham area had a basic but honest homelife. Mothers were the focal point for most families as many fathers were away fighting or working all hours of the day and night, on the home front.

Mums, therefore, did their best to make the home as comfortable and secure as they could. Many mothers extended their families and welcomed in the troops who were parked up in the roads ready for D-Day. Meagre rations were made to go a long way by ingenuity and great resourcefulness. Cooking hints churned out by the Ministry of Food, told mothers how to successfully use dried eggs and make the most of their sugar ration.

'Meat cakes without fat', 'Fatless dumplings' and 'Mock suet pudding' with jam or syrup, were just some of the recipes that mothers were encouraged to dish out to their families.

Gardens were no longer places for just flowers and a neat lawn. They were areas of cultivation and most families became good at growing their own vegetables. No garden was allowed to become overgrown and useless, for with food in such short supply, every plot had to make a contribution.

Against this back-drop of austerity, Fareham families got on with their lives and somehow managed to keep smiling.

Mrs Phyl Manuel, lived with her young daughter, Jennifer, at Wallington. Her husband was in the forces and only returned sporadically during the length of the war. Her mother lived with her some of the time and while life may have seemed quite difficult, she just got used to the hardships of wartime.

"We only had one main general shop in Fareham and that was the International Stores in West Street. There was a butchers in West Street that I used as well – with the ration book you got used to going to just one place. Toys were very scarce. I think my daughter had dolls but they were probably second-hand. I remember buying a second-hand pram for her, from somebody in Portchester and I think there was a doll as well. I remember one of my sisters-in-law, who was a nurse in London, coming home with a teddy bear which she had acquired.

"Clothes were also scarce. I made a lot of things – I used to sew and knit but shoes were a real problem because they were part of the clothes ration. Children's shoes were particularly difficult because they kept growing out of them. You would go to the shoe shop and keep asking for them and they would tell you if they were expecting anything in. I remember one particular shoe shop in the West Street in Fareham, called Corbins and if they had a new pair of shoes for children or adults, they would put one pair of shoes in the window and you would just hope it was the size you wanted.

"They were like gold dust but you just can't imagine it now."

D-Day itself has a special significance for Mrs Manuel. Her husband was home on leave and the couple went for a cosy drink at the local pub. It was here that Mrs Manuel heard a distinctive voice that was to give her a clue that something was afoot.

"My husband was on embarkation leave on D-day and he went soon after that to Ceylon. The night before D-day, he and I went down for a drink at the Red Lion in Fareham and that was absolutely full of military personnel. One particular person was there, I remember , he was a radio reporter called Howard Marshall and he had a very distinctive voice – I recognised him from the voice.

"It was quite a jolly atmosphere in there and everyone was rushing about. It was very

Phyl Manuel with daughter, Jennifer

obvious that something was up because the pub was absolutely packed.

"On actual D-Day, we went to Droxford by train on the Meon Valley line and we met up with my brother-in-law and his fiancee. As we walked from the station, we could see the planes and gliders, I suppose it was the middle of the morning, going out across Portsmouth."

───────── ◆ ─────────

Mrs Freda Triggs, from Titchfield, has special memories of D-Day. Her sister had come to live at her Derlyn Road home, after a time bomb had been found in her sister's garden.

"Friends of my sister who were in the army, came to the door on the evening before D-Day. They said they were going over tomorrow but they couldn't tell us what time. We made some tea and sandwiches and all sat round chatting. Then my sister asked one of them, who was called David, `When was the last time you washed your socks?'

"He said he didn't really know, but thought it was a week or two. So my sister said `For goodness sake, all of you take your socks off and we'll wash them for you.' It was a nice evening and after we had washed the socks we hung all of them out on the line to dry.

"Then David, who my sister knew because he had been billeted with her family, suggested we should all go for a drink. We went to the Gordon Arms and my husband stayed home to look after my son. When we came back we had a cup of coffee, cakes and sandwiches. By then it was time for them to go. We kissed them all goodbye and I didn't know one or two of them from Adam.

"The next day, my sister and I went down and stood at the top of Portland Street to watch all the soldiers going by. I had my son with me in his pram and we stood there waving to them all as they went by but we never saw David or any of the others.

"We knew there were a lot of troops in Fareham but we hadn't seen them in all the roads. When you went out shopping, you always hurried home as fast as you could in case there was an air raid.

"We were short of food but we learned to get by and people seemed happier in lots of ways. There was much more companionship."

───────── ◆ ─────────

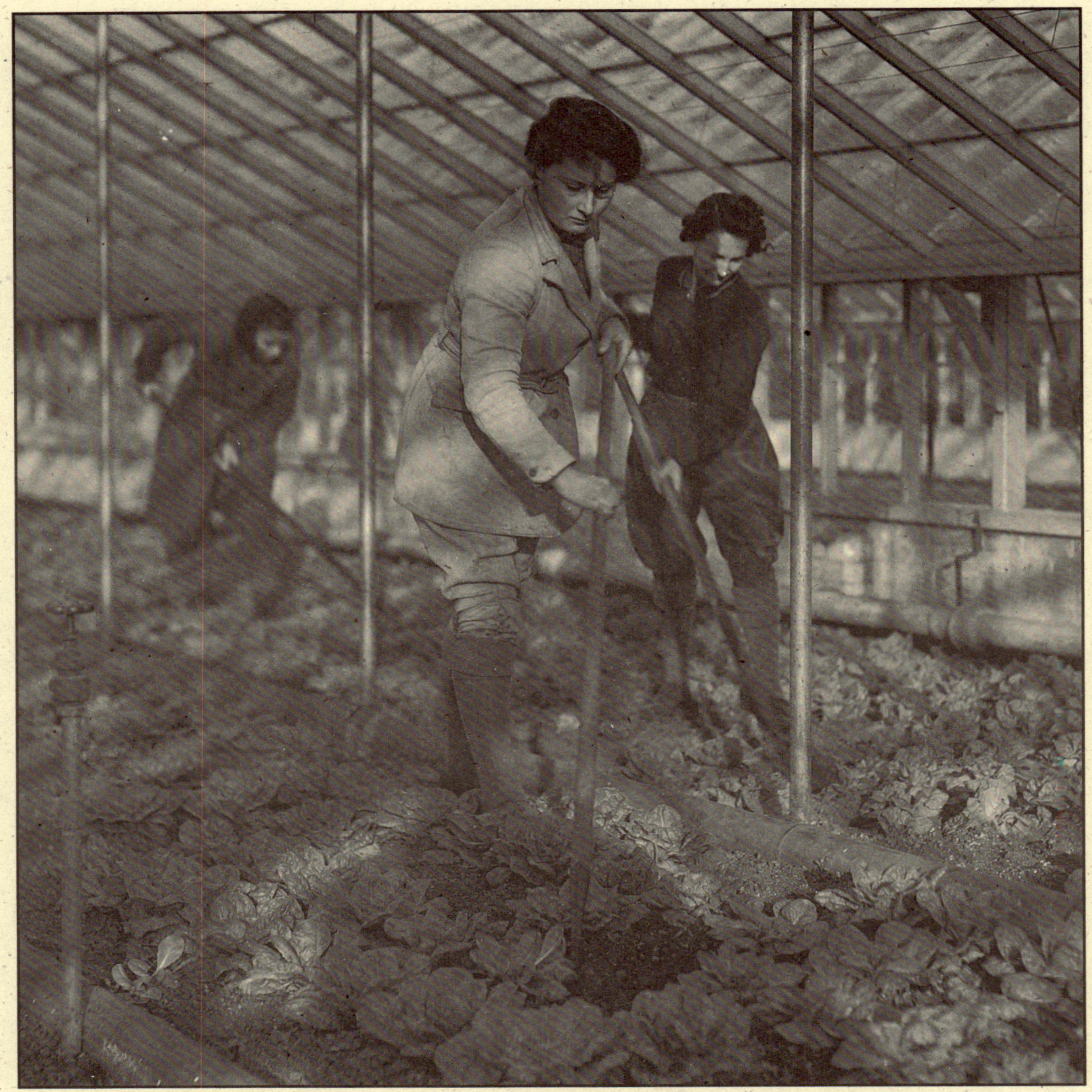

Mrs Olly Pepperell, worked on the land with her sister, growing vegetables for the forces at Westcote Nurseries in Cyprus Road, Locks Heath. She was newly married, running her home in Warsash Road and working hard for the war effort. Dressed in her special issue dungarees, she worked at the greenhouses, tending the seedlings. The work was generally enjoyable and it was only the bitter cold which sometimes made it unpleasant.

"The agricultural rations that we got once a month were a real treat. You were given cheese because they reckoned it helped you work and all these things like margarine, a bit of lard and tea. We used to come home with a 12lb basket and we used to say `goodee we've got our rations.'

"We used to start work at about seven thirty in the morning and it used to be so cold. But we were lucky because we had made coats out of these lovely tweedy blankets that the Commando's had given us. When people saw that coat they used to ask how many coupons it had taken to buy it...

"You had to have the black market, you couldn't exist without it. I remember this one time, I was in the Jolly Farmer pub with my husband having a drink, when a sailor I knew from HMS Tormentor edged up to me and said in a whisper `I've got a nice blanket'. So I asked him where it was and he said it was out in the rabbit hutch outside the pub. So we went to have a look at it and it was a lovely white blanket. I asked him how much he wanted for it and he said five bob – so we bought it."

A special relationship existed between the personnel at HMS Tormentor, Warsash and the families in the surrounding communities. The local mothers were happy to help where they could and the deals that were struck were beneficial to both sides.

"I used to do washing for some of the Chief Petty Officers at Tormentor. They would bring their stuff on a Sunday and stay for tea. Then they would come to collect their washing during the week. When they asked how much they owed me for doing it, I said I didn't want any money but if you can get a bit of tea, we would be more than pleased.

"So they used to come here with a packet of tea for us. Then one day, I was asked by one of the men on the landing craft, if I could make a Christmas cake and if so, they would supply the ingredients. So three of them came to the house and I said – they looked as if they had put on some weight. And then it all came out from under their jackets – currants, sultanas, raisins, eggs, demerara sugar, they had the best of everything.

"I made them a huge cake for 22 of them and when they gave the Captain a piece, he asked them where they had got it. My friend said Mrs Pepperell made it and the Captain said 'Gosh, she must be in the know' – but I reckon he knew what was going on.

"The day they brought all the stuff was my son Roy's birthday. So they said to make him a cake as well and asked if they could come to his party. They asked if I could make a trifle for the party and said they would bring the stuff. Sure enough, they brought the sponge cakes and the fruit for a trifle and they said it was lovely to sit down at a white tablecloth."

Cooking for the family on a day to day basis could be something of a trial. Mrs Pepperell, like many other mothers, was faced with the task of making the best of the basic ingredients available. Her imagination was tested to the full but she can still recall some of her culinary triumphs.

"If I was lucky enough to get sausages, I would put them in the oven and cook them. Then I mixed up this batter but it never had an egg in it – because you couldn't afford to use them like that. The batter was made from flour and a tiny drop of milk, water, with a little bit of bicarbonate to make it rise – and you had to eat it as soon as it came out of the oven.

"Another thing we used to do which made me laugh, was a recipe with parsnips. We used to grow them ourselves and then cook them, mash them up and put in banana flavouring. My husband and son Roy, used to think they were eating banana sandwiches. Roy used to brag to his friends 'We've had banana sandwiches' and all the mothers would come running down to ask me where I got the bananas from.

"Another thing I used to make, involved mashing up carrots and swedes together and then rolling them in flour and frying them. And they used to say what's this – so I told them it was rissoles – but it didn't have any meat in. We must have been healthy though in those days. When we were working in the fields we would munch a carrot or chop off a swede, peel it and eat it. "We used to queue for everything in the shops. If someone told you there were bananas at a certain shop, you would rush round there and join the queue. One day I saw a queue and I thought, I'd better join it even though I didn't know what it was for. It turned out it was for jelly – and I queued for about half an hour for that one jelly."

To relieve the tedium of war, Mrs Pepperell used to go to the cinema. Her husband, who was naturally worried for her safety, was not keen on these outings to Southampton and told her, not to go!

But when her niece wanted to see the film 'Over the Rainbow', she agreed to take her – as long as they kept it a secret from Mr Pepperell. However, the film show did not stay secret for long.

Her young niece was inadvertently singing the catchy theme tune to the film, when Mr Pepperell overheard her. He asked where she had heard it and she blurted out that she had been to the cinema with her aunt...and Mr Pepperell was not best pleased.

"*Butter, Madam?—Would you please join the queue!*"

"My husband was a shipwright in Southampton docks, it was a reserved occupation. He used to cycle from Warsash Road to Southampton docks and sometimes I wouldn't see him for two or three days – he had to work so hard.

"He was in the Home Guard in Locks Heath, just like Dad's Army. I was in the ARP and used to do the stirrup pump. We were a team of three and my sister used to run with buckets of water and the other one was supplying her. We used to scream with laughter when we were on exercises. We were trained to put out incendiary bombs but we were very fortunate because we never had to do it for real."

D-Day is a bitter sweet memory for Mrs Pepperell. She can still recall the build up of military personnel around her home as if it were yesterday and she can remember worrying for the safety of her own brother who took part in the invasion.

"When we saw all these tanks in Park Gate, right down along Station Road, nose to tail almost, we used to think – well, what on earth is going on, why are they there?

"But it was a well kept secret. On the actual day, I was in the greenhouse watering and all of a sudden there was no water and I thought I had a leak in the hosepipe. A voice called my name, when I looked round it was my brother and he said to come on home as they had landed over the other side and he would soon be going. He had an army motorbike, so I got on the back and we went home. We had a cup of tea with my Mum, who was also there – then he said cheerio and off he went. He went straight over and within a week he was back.

"I had a card from the Army, to say he was shot right through the chest and out the back. All the things we had sent to him were sent back directly. I had sent him a big home-made cake and even that was sent back.

"They told me he was in Netley Hospital, so I went by bike from Locks Heath up to Netley. When I got there I had never seen such chaos in all my life. There were bodies everywhere, I wanted to get my coat off and do something. The Sister came out and said my brother had just gone, about half an hour ago. I thought she meant he was dead but then she explained, that they had dressed his wounds and sent him to a hospital right in the North.

"He was alright and he's still alive – he's 85 and as upright as ever he was."

Mrs Joan Collins, from Warsash, has lived in the village since she was a young girl. She married in 1935 and her daughter, Jane, was born three years later. Her husband ran the Clock Tower garage (now known as Roxby Garage) and the local taxi service – he did not join up for military service until the end of the war.

"There was plenty of taxi work. He had various lads from HMS Tormentor who were taxi drivers. They used to come up into the flat and play pontoon and solo, waiting for taxi jobs to come in. If one of them had to go off on a taxi job, I would take over their hand but I never really could play cards all that well.

"My husband was a speedway rider originally. His father was the local butcher. My husband ran the garage right on through the war until about 1943 and then an uncle of mine, who had been in London, retired and he came into the business to take over the office work.

"In the end when my husband did join up, he was based at Lee on Solent, so he came home every night and carried on the business with my uncle."

The Collins family lived above the garage premises. They had moved there in about 1943 and Mrs Collins can remember they had their first television set then.

"It was a horrible picture by today's standard but we thought it was wonderful. I didn't really listen to the radio, I used to have the television on for company and we read the local papers."

People living in the community were expected to do their bit and for about nine months Mrs Collins, along with other local women, carried out fire watch duties.

"We were issued with a tin helmet and I remember standing on the front door step for hours on end. I used to pop upstairs and make a cuppa and take it down with me. In the end I took a chair down to sit on but nothing ever happened.

"My husband was in the Home Guard, I remember he was issued with some sort of uniform. The Victory Hall was taken over as a first aid post and my sister, my sister-in-law and my aunt were all involved with the ARP."

Like many mothers, Mrs Collins became skilled in needle craft and learned to transform old clothes into new garments.

"I used to cut up my husband's trousers, to make skirts for my daughter and I made a coat for myself out of a blanket. I had been brought up to make clothes so we coped very well. We used curtain fabric for all sorts of things and we used to knit a lot, when we could get the wool.

"With my husband being in the trade, he made my daughter a bike out of bits. I can remember him putting blocks on the pedals because she wasn't very old and couldn't reach them properly.

"He found an old saddle somewhere that didn't really fit but it had to do."

Warsash attracted its fair share of celebrities from stage and screen. Most of them were either based at nearby HMS Tormentor or would appear in shows at the base. The locals became used to seeing these stars on their streets and treated them as part of the local community.

"Ralph Richardson was at Tormentor and Anne Shelton used to come here because she was going out with David Reid, who was also at Tormentor. Vivien Leigh used to come to our back door at the Tower Garage for my husband to change a cheque for her. She would always have a scarf tied round her head."

Due to the shortage of basic and luxury items, the black market economy flourished at this time and it was always handy to be acquainted with 'someone in the know.'

"There used to be a man who came round from Southampton and he started off bringing meat – it was black market stuff, I think. He used to come to my front door of an evening and one day he brought some combs. You couldn't buy a comb anywhere and these were quite reasonable so I bought two dozen of them and sold them to all my friends.

"My husband also knew a man who kept pigs and he used to have all the swill from the Army – and what went out of the swill was nobody's business. He used to come in with great big tins of corned beef, things like that went out in the pig swill and were put on the black market. It was tinned stuff so it didn't matter, the labels might be a bit odd but what was inside was okay.

"I also remember somebody coming once

and bringing a suit and that must have been `hot.' I think I bought it for about five pounds, it was a coat and skirt in a grey pinstripe. It was very smart but I was half afraid to wear it.

"I guessed it was `hot', I didn't know where it had come from and I didn't ask."

◆

Mrs Lou Webb, lived at Lower Swanwick. She was staying with her mother and father at the time of D-Day because her father, who was the head of the first aid post at Park Gate, was unwell.

"We had tanks right outside the house waiting for D-Day and the Canadians on the tanks used to come into our place every day. I would cook them breakfast and they used to wash and shave.

"While they were with us, they would tell us about their homes. My young son David would have been about two or three years old at that time and they gave him a lovely baseball. He has still got it to this day – and he treasures it very much indeed.

"It made a great deal of difference having the troops there because you were on edge all the time, wondering what was going to happen next.

"While the tanks were all parked up here, the first Doodlebug in this country landed at Park Gate – where the library is now – it was a spare piece of land in those days. When it came down and exploded, some of it fell on a tank and `set off' all the ammunition that was loaded on it. The soldiers were in a house close by, playing cards and one of them rushed out in his stocking feet and jumped in his tank and drove it away to a spare piece of land – so it wouldn't do any more harm."

It is often assumed that Fareham did not suffer major attacks from enemy aircraft. But the area had its fair share of dramas and did not escape the incendiary attacks, which had wrought so much damage elsewhere.

"One night the flak was so dense, they couldn't get in to bomb Portsmouth so they dropped the incendiaries all along the railway line here, the last two landed in a Damson tree, right outside our back door."

◆

Mrs Winifred Bynam, was a near neighbour of Mrs Webb and the two women are still friends to this day. She, too, was surrounded by Canadian troops and their tanks.

"Those troops that were out on the road, we invited in for baths and some of them slept in a tent on our lawn. Occasionally we all had a game of cards. They were here for about three weeks and during that time my mother and father moved in with me.

"My father was head gardener on the Brooklands estate and they had to turn out of their cottage and move in with me for those three weeks. They needed a permit every time they wanted to get back into their house.

"We had a Morrison shelter in the sitting room and they made that their home for the time they were with me. We knew something was up because they had been moved out but my parents never said to me whether they had been told anything about D-Day."

Mrs Bynam, can remember waking up on D-Day, to discover all the troops had vanished and after all the hustle and bustle, there was suddenly an air of calm.

"After D-Day, we had a pageant at Brooklands, to celebrate D-Day. It was held in front of the house and the people who came to watch stood on the terraces. Those who took part represented different countries and I was Norway."

◆

As Britain prepared for the D-Day landings, Mrs Doris Cox, from Fareham, was waiting for her own momentous occasion.....the birth of her first child.

Her husband was away in the services and Mrs Cox had given up a career as a writer and later as a psychologist's writer in the Wrens at HMS Collingwood, when motherhood beckoned. During the months of waiting, she

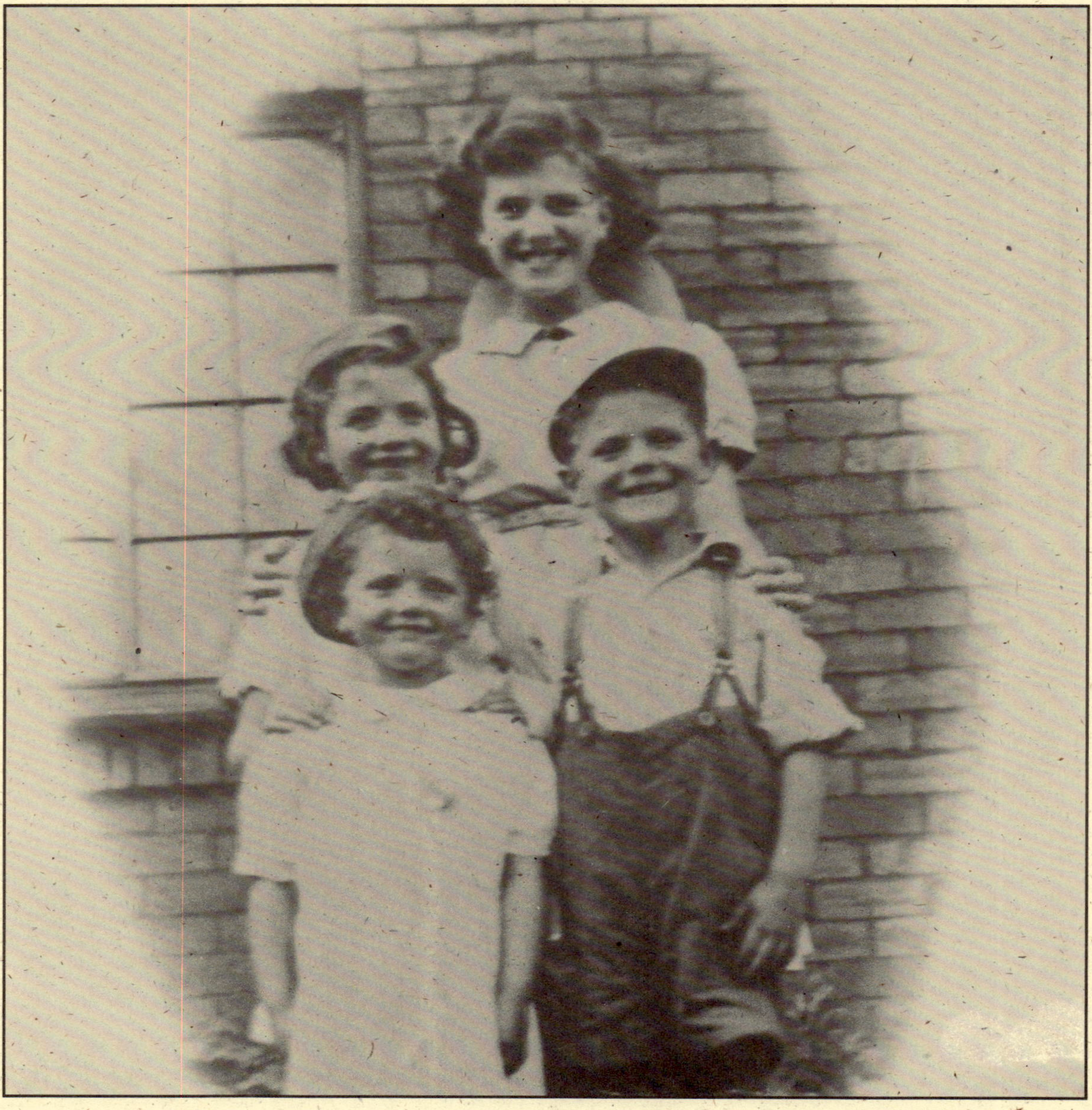

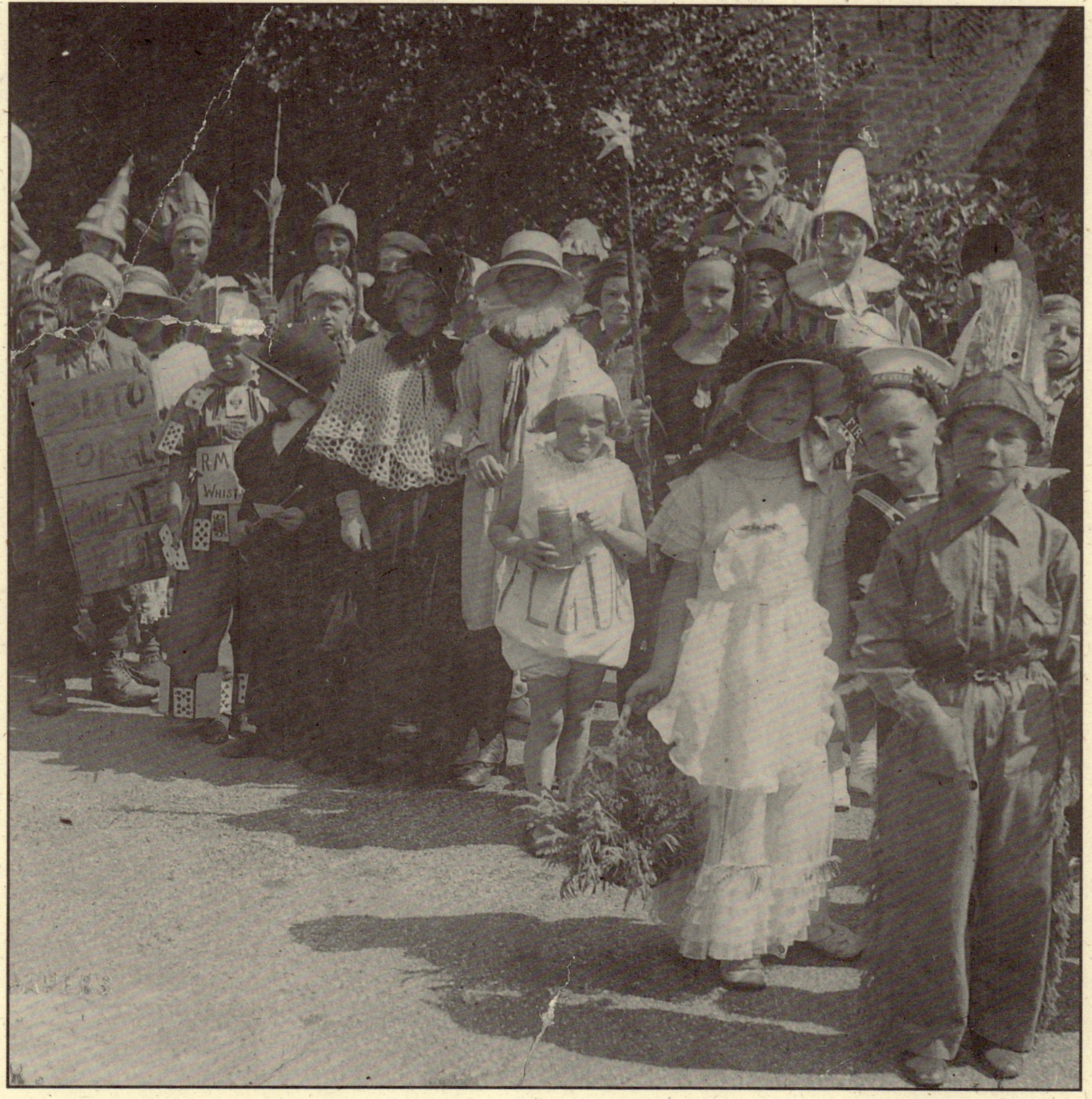

lived at home with her parents in Westborn Road and kept herself busy knitting clothes for the new arrival.

"When I was at home waiting for the baby to be born, friends gave me wool and I did some knitting. I was no good at sewing so the only thing I made was nappies. We bought some towelling and I used the sewing machine to make them. My mother had kept some of my baby clothes and they were very useful.

"Before I went into hospital, the road outside my house was full of tanks and armoured vehicles. Everybody made the troops some tea and bits to eat. The soldiers would try to make it up to us with things in kind, like giving us sweets and things like that.

"There was a lot of comradeship in those days and it did help to make you feel better. You knew that those lads were away from their families and your own family was away as well, so you knew how each other felt. In a way, it was reassuring having them outside your house but then you did wonder if they would be a target for the Germans. But it was very exciting to live through."

The time came for Mrs Cox to go into hospital, to have her baby and she had her fair share of adventures on the ward.

"My son, Anthony, was born on May 14 1944 in St Mary's Hospital, Portsmouth. The baby was early and shouldn't have been born in May but I had some complications.

"I was in hospital for three months altogether and there were a lot of raids over Portsmouth at that time. On the run-up to D-Day, my son had already been born and I remember they emptied as many wards as they could and sent people home, ready to receive the casualties they were expecting. But they kept me in and moved me to another ward – I came home in mid June.

"Considering the shortages we were going through, it was very good in the hospital. They gave us a lot of care and whenever there were raids they used to say to most of the patients 'get under your bed'. But they wouldn't let me get under there because they thought it was too dangerous for me to move. So I had to just lie in my bed and hope the ceiling wouldn't come down on me."

Some things, it seems, never change and while the care she received during her stay in hospital was faultless, the same could not be said of the food. On the whole, it was pretty unappetising and it was only when friends or relatives brought in some goodies that Mrs Cox felt like tucking in – and naturally she shared her treats with her fellow patients and nurses.

"The food in hospital was appalling, we had sago pudding one day and rice pudding the next. It just went on and on, sago or rice. It was quite difficult to have variety and I remember when I was waiting to have my baby, my mother brought me a little rhubarb tart, with rhubarb she had grown in the garden and everybody wanted some.

"A friend of my husband's came back from South Africa and he brought in a box of bananas. Of course everyone went wild because we hadn't seen bananas since before the war, so I shared them out with all the patients and nurses on the ward."

At home, Mrs Cox and her baby son, soon adjusted to the new routine. But there were no little luxuries to ease the hardship – you made do with what you had or went without.

"When I came home from hospital, I had my mother to help me. My husband was down in Plymouth and he got home fairly often. After the baby was weaned, it was very difficult to get suitable food. I remember paying half a crown for a few carrots to make a bit of stew for him – and in those days that was a lot of money.

"You got your ration of powdered milk, orange juice and cod liver oil. Whenever there was anything extra, they used to try to give it to people with young babies. The baby clothing was utility and very plain, not pretty at all. I used to long for the pretty clothes I had seen with smocking... and that sort of thing.

"Friends would knit things for me and we made bedding from things we tore up. We made cot sheets from bigger sheets and baby blankets from those that had seen better days.

"We had to order a pram and because my mother was superstitious she wouldn't have it at home until after the baby was born. There was a shop in Fareham called Keasts in West Street and they saved a pram for me. Originally they had a lot of baby things in the shop but by 1944 they had sold most of what they had and it was very difficult to get anything for babies. My father made wooden toys and if you couldn't get other things that you wanted, you just went without."

——————— ◆ ———————

FIVE

There's an old saying 'Hard work never did anyone any harm,' and if the people of Fareham are anything to go by, this saying is certainly true. Fareham people were used to working from half past seven in the morning until as late as 8 o' clock at night – then spending the remaining hours of the day on fire watch, home guard or air raid duties. Often, they went straight from their night duties to their day job – with only a quick cuppa to revive their tired bones. Maybe the passage of time has blurred their recollections of this routine 24 hour day – but there is no denying that life at that time was indeed tough.

It's ironic, that people were working harder than ever on a restricted diet – but the experience seemingly left them unscathed. For some it was all work and no play – but others still have happy memories of the odd night out at the cinema or local dance. It was the feeling of 'everyone being in the same boat' which helped Fareham people through these hard times.

The main concern was for the day when peace would come and life would be orderly once more. This was the motivating factor and gave people something to look forward to. They could put up with all the hard work because they knew that at the end of the day they were contributing to the war effort.

It was an especially important time for women. They became essential to the war effort by taking over jobs which had traditionally been in the male domain. Factory and agricultural work became a way of life for women and they were a dominant force on the production line. The work was repetitive and tedious but very necessary to the war effort and that made the toil all the more worthwhile.

Mrs Margaret Beckett, was a prime example. She worked at the Fleetlands factory near Fareham, repairing planes that had been damaged in battle. She was called up to do the work and saw it as her duty. She had no other life for virtually the whole of the war. Her husband was away fighting, so she lived alone and dealt with all the problems which presented themselves during those long, hard years.

"I had to work at Fleetlands. I had a letter from the Ministry of Labour telling me where to go and you didn't argue – you just had to go.

"I was a cleaner, at the Embassy Cinema in Fareham when I was called up. At Fleetlands, I started off as a cleaner, sweeping the floors and things like that but I was only on it for about a month and then they moved me up and I had to be a cleaner on the aircraft parts. From there, I moved up to learning to be an aircraft fitter and that meant repairing the parts that came off the damaged planes so they could be re-used. We worked on helicopters, Spitfires and all sorts of planes."

Mrs Beckett became used to her new work routine and her job became central to her life – whether she liked it or not.

"It wasn't a case of enjoying the work – you just got used to it. I would leave my home in Wallington, at six forty-five in the morning, and I worked from seven thirty until half past six in the evening. You were supposed to finish at four thirty in the afternoon but you always had to do two hours overtime.

"You had one Saturday afternoon off a month. We worked six days a week normally but we did manage to get Sundays off, thank goodness. I never went out much and on the Sunday, I always had to do a little bit of housework at home. I had to rely on the neighbours to take my milk in and on the coalman to leave me a hundred weight of coal if and when he had it. But very often, I never bothered to have a fire because by the time I had lit it, it was time for me to go to bed – to be ready for work the next day."

The warmest spot on the coldest day is BOVRIL

Nothing takes the nip out of the wind like Bovril. It warms the very cockles of your heart and puts new strength into you as well. This is a time when good health is essential. Keep fit—keep cheery on Hot Bovril.

There were just as many women as men working at Fleetlands. Mrs Beckett's job demanded a steady hand and she had to pass a tough practical examination before being allowed to work on the aircraft.

"They gave you a part of a wing that was damaged and you had to drill the holes out of that and it went through to the inspection department, to see if you had done it right. And then you had to show that you could drill out all the old rivets, which weren't much bigger than the head of a pin and you couldn't let your drill wander. You had to show them three different pieces and if you passed that test, they upgraded you.

"Fleetlands was run by the Ministry of Defence and there were people from all over working there. There were one or two from Dorset who came to work there. They would billet the people who weren't local and they would stay in Fareham and go home at weekends."

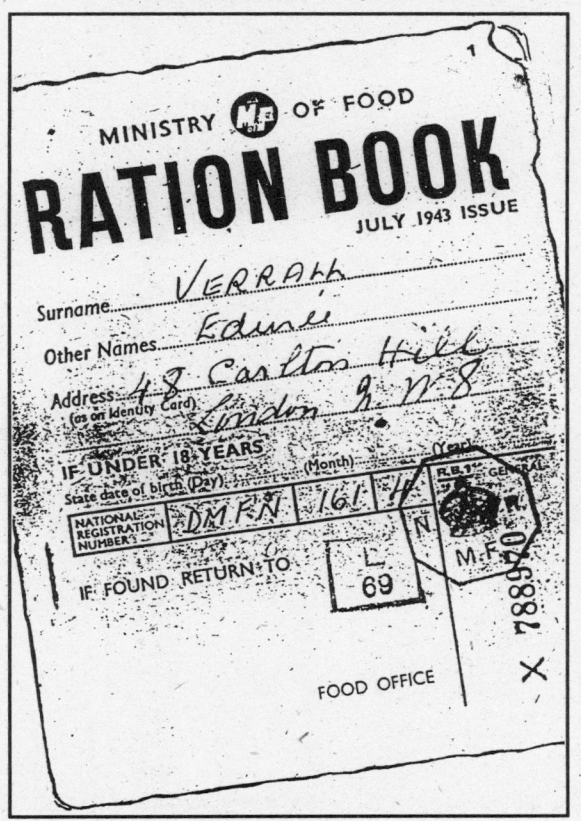

Pay day was every Friday but it was not really a cause for celebration. These were not big earning days and most workers had just enough to get by and no more.

"We were paid about £15 to £20 a month, which wasn't that much. We had to clock in and if you were a minute late you would lose a quarter of an hour's pay. If you were off sick, you would lose a bit of your wages and you weren't supposed to take a day off unless it was absolutely necessary – but you did get an annual holiday of a fortnight.

"We had Good Friday, Easter Monday and days like that off. You looked forward to those days off because it gave you a little break.

And if your husband was home on leave, you could have time off but you didn't get any pay, obviously.

"I never went anywhere on my holiday because my husband was away in the Army but I used to take the time off to have a break from work.

"I used to live on the money that I was earning and bank my husband's Army allowance which was about thirty shillings a week. It was a hard life but you thought that everyone else was the same as you, so you put up with it and you didn't grumble.

"It was a long day and the overtime was compulsory. I wouldn't say the work was hard but it was monotonous. Can you imagine sitting on the wing of a plane and drilling out all day long – and the noise, of course, was atrocious.

"You had a quarter of an hour's break in the morning and the same in the afternoon.

"And then, I would cycle home, which would take me about twenty minutes, if there was nothing on the roads."

Getting to and from work was a real adventure for Mrs Beckett. She travelled by bicycle and had to take her chances on the road, weaving in and out of the tanks – hoping they would spot the feeble ray of light thrown out by her cycle lamps.

"Coming up to D-Day, it was worse than ever on the roads. The tanks would come down from Wickham Road and the ones who were going to Portsmouth would go down Wallington Hill over the old bridge.

"Trying to fight your way through that lot at night, with a little tiny lamp on your bike, with cardboard on it, to make sure the light shone on the road, was horrific really. And I used to have to cycle through all the smoke from the smoke screen lorries, but I got used to it in the end.

"I look back now and think, how did I ever manage it because I used to wake up before six in the morning, to get to work on time – especially if it was pouring with rain."

There were times when Mrs Beckett would not get any sleep for 48 hours at a time. If there was an air raid on when she got home from work in the evening, she would go to the local shelter and rest as best she could – but she rarely managed to sleep on these occasions. Lack of sleep, however, was only one of the problems she had to overcome.

Managing to get enough food was a continual battle. The rationing system, which was meant to ensure everyone received their fair share, was fine in theory but in reality – if you were working six days a week, during normal shop hours, it often meant that you went without food.

"Sometimes, I would come home from work and go straight to the shelter and be there all night long. Then I would come back home in the morning, make myself a cup of tea and go off to work. I didn't get a quarter of the rations I was entitled to because by the time I got up to the shops it was all sold out. You didn't get anything saved for you.

"Whatever food came into the town, you didn't have a chance of getting because all the people who weren't working got there first. I had some relatives who would give me a lunch at the weekend and there was a canteen at Fleetlands. But if you didn't get there early enough, you didn't get anything there either. There were thousands of people working there and they only had a certain amount of food to go round.

"One got used to it, if you didn't get to the canteen in time, that was just your bad luck. Quite often I didn't get anything at all! My sister-in-law, used to try to get me a loaf of bread so I could take a sandwich with me, just in case I missed out.

"The war was something that I wouldn't have missed. It was a real experience and an experience that I think would do a lot of people good today – because they have it all so easy now, and have everything given to them on a plate."

───────── ◆ ─────────

Mr Vernon Lees, is only too aware of the important – but mostly unsung – role that civilians played during the war years. The former Fareham Council architect saw it from both sides – as an engineer working on wartime craft for Vospers, the shipbuilders and as an Airman with the RAF... and on balance he believes that life was a lot tougher on `civvy street.'

He worked on the torpedo boats and the important Mulberry Harbour project but his working day did not finish when he left the Vospers shipyard.

As soon as Mr Lees got home to his digs in the evening, he had to change into his Home Guard uniform and prepare to go on duty throughout the night.

Ironically, the anti-aircraft gun that Mr Lees used to man at North Wallington was positioned only a matter of yards away from his home today.

"We used to start work at Vospers at seven thirty in the morning and finish any time after seven at night. Then I would cycle home and change into my Home Guard uniform – and be on duty until seven thirty the next morning.

"It was like this day in and day out. I was only 18 or 19 years old and you can do an awful lot more when you are a teenager – no one ever complained.

"It's strange because I was a very keen dancer and even though I was so busy, I always found time to go and dance – let off steam and have a few pints."

The Vospers yard was forced to move to Portchester, after its premises in Portsmouth were devastated during a bombing raid.

"THERE'S BEEN A SERIOUS INCIDENT AT POST 14. SOMEBODY'S SWIPED THE OXO!"

76

"When they had the Blitz in Portsmouth, I went down on duty and I didn't leave for two days. Then I went into Vospers and started cleaning up ready for the move to Portchester."

It was at times such as this that everyone was expected to do their bit and most people had at least two jobs. Mr Lees can still remember one colleague at Vospers, who fell foul of the law when he failed to turn up for Home Guard duty.

"Someone saw him in the Railway Inn pub and because he didn't turn up for duty he was court marshalled by the Army and sent to the military prison or `glass house' as it was known, at Aldershot. When he came back he was absolutely useless for work for weeks."

---◆---

Working at Lukes Yard on the River Hamble, Mr Dick Marshall, from Dibles Road, Warsash, had the perfect vantage point for viewing the build-up to D-Day.

He worked on the landing craft, which were to play such a crucial role in the D-Day landings, as well as carrying out other essential work for the Royal Navy.

"Hamble River began to prepare for D-Day from early 1943, with the continued expansion of HMS Tormentor at Warsash and the building of the shore base HMS Cricket, above the railway bridge at Bursledon.

"HMS Tormentor had had a large number of small USA built R. boats reclassed as LCPs (Landing Craft Personnel) from late 1940, but now began to assemble a large fleet of 105ft LCI's (Landing Craft Infantry) which had been built mainly on the East Coast of England and were capable of crossing the English Channel under their own power, when fully loaded.

"These LCIs required larger crews and more facilities, which meant a new jetty had to be constructed outside of the crab pond and the RAF jetty head had to be modified.

"Two small steam tugs were now also allocated to HMS Tormentor and stationed at the river entrance. The US Army now also started to arrive on the river. They constructed a base for a Port Maintenance Unit, on mudland that they reclaimed adjacent to Hamble Quay. This was for the repair of all their harbour barges and tugboats.

"All the shipyards on the river helped in the D-Day preparations, mainly with work on landing craft etc. We at Lukes Yard repaired and re-engined many landing craft of all types ready for D-Day, as well as carrying on with our regular work for the Royal Navy.

"HMS Cricket soon became operational with Royal Marine and Royal Navy personnel. On most days, their LCAs (Landing Craft Assault) and Ambulance Launches could be seen proceeding in and out of the river on training exercises. HMS Tormentor's new LCIs were also busy, training and practising landings at Lepe and Stokes Bay. As 1944 progressed, more and more different British, Canadian and American units arrived in the locality, setting up camp on village greens and other suitable sites. This gave everyone the feeling that some large operation was going to commence in the very near future.

"We in the Home Guard had extra night guard duties and I well remember one night, just prior to D-Day, when I was in charge of the guard on Bursledon Railway bridge and a large explosion occurred just to the east. An Army despatch rider, who stopped at our post shortly afterwards, told me that a large bomb had landed on some Canadian tanks and equipment parked further up the road, at Park Gate.

"It was a short time after this, while towing a patrol boat up Southampton Water in daylight, that we were overtaken by a small, noisy, flying object, which disappeared in the direction of Southampton. This was the V1 flying bomb that I saw and they now began to pass over and crash and explode in ever increasing numbers. I later found out that the explosion that I had heard while on Bursledon railway bridge, had been the first V1 to land in Britain. We received orders not to attempt to shoot them down with small arms fire.

"While we were working on the river during June 5, we observed many troops embarking on HMS Tormentor's LCIs from the jetties at Warsash. We then knew that D-Day was imminent and that these were the spearhead troops embarking.

"The next day, June 6, the river off Warsash was very quiet with all the LCIs having sailed to take part in the D-Day landings in France. The only vessels in immediate view, when looking down and out of the river, were some coastal tankers belonging to the fleet that was being assembled and which were lying at anchor outside of the main entrance.

"These tankers did not commence to operate until a short time later, when the small port of Port-en-Bassin was liberated.

———————— ◆ ————————

Mr Claude Daish, joined Fairey Aviation as the war started and each day cycled from his home at Sarisbury Green to Warsash where he crossed the river to get to work. He was aged 19 in 1944 and lived in the house next to the pub which is now called Flat Foot Sams.

Mr Daish, in common with most of the people working on the home front, was no stranger to hard work. He became used to a seven day week – with only one Saturday and Sunday off, once every month. Despite the long hours spent at work, he had time to see the build-up of troops around his home.

"As it got closer to D-Day, the whole of Sarisbury Green became a camp – for men brought in to maintain the service vehicles. From Bursledon Bridge to Park Gate, there were Canadian tanks at the side of the road. They were parked so close to the pavement that when they swung their guns round they would often hit the side of the house. Behind the Parish Rooms at Sarisbury, there was a petrol dump. The River Hamble got so congested in the run-up to D-Day, they used to say that you could have walked across without getting your feet wet."

As well as working at Fairey's factory, Mr Daish was in the Home Guard and carried out his duties at Titchfield Hill, the main Telephone Exchange at Fareham and at Vospers shipyard.

"We used to train near Stokes Bay, using live ammunition and throwing hand grenades. All of a sudden, from being just an ordinary village youth, you were a full grown man carrying a machine gun around.

"We would get home from work, have our tea and get changed for Home Guard duty. The Army would take us to where we were on duty. You would do an hour's duty and then sleep in a tent until the morning, when the Army would come and get you again. I had enough time to say hello to my mother, have some breakfast and then cycle to work. I started at seven thirty in the morning and finished at 7 o' clock at night, working on Fairey Fireflys. We would repair damaged planes and make parts for new ones.

"We didn't have much of a social life. Dances were held at Sarisbury Green Parish Rooms and I would go there and occasionally, I would go to the cinema. But mostly I went home to sleep."

Mr Daish, had a twin brother and he can still recall the excitement they both felt, growing up during the war years.

"At that age, we were more excited by what was going on than feeling frightened. When the sirens went off, our mother used to tell us to go in the shelter but we used to stand outside and watch the bombing.

"The soldiers had lots of food on them before D-day, I can remember the Canadian troops handing us huge bags of bacon before they left.

"We had no idea when D-Day was going to happen but we knew that something was going on."

The war changed many people's lives forever. Families were often torn apart and the sad loss of loved ones, left a deep emotional scar that, for many, made life in the '40's a matter of sheer survival.

However, on top of these dramatic personal changes, the war changed the way people viewed the world and more importantly the way they looked upon their own environment.

"Friendship in those days was altogether different. Prior to the war we all lived a village life and didn't really travel far. If you went to Hayling Island for instance, you would go by charabanc and it would take all day to get there and back and a trip to London was something you looked forward to for months.

"During the war people moved out from Southampton and settled in places like Sarisbury, Locks Heath, Titchfield and Warsash. The war altered village life from the word go – and it would never be the same again."

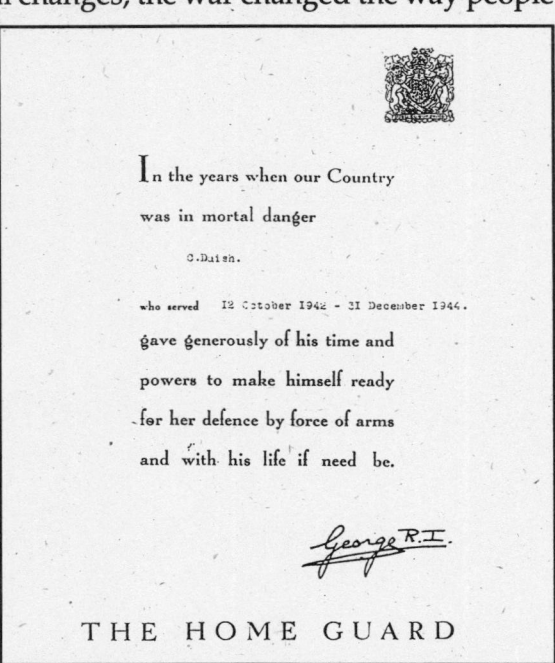

In the years when our Country was in mortal danger

G. Daish.

who served   12 October 1942 - 31 December 1944.

gave generously of his time and powers to make himself ready for her defence by force of arms and with his life if need be.

George R.I.

THE HOME GUARD

> **Hi! old boy... SAVE THAT BONE FOR SALVAGE... don't bury it!**
>
> "What? This old bone? It's all gnawed to bits." "*That* doesn't matter. Master says, to shorten the war we've got to salvage every scrap of bone we can. He says bones help make Glue for Aircraft construction... and Glycerine for Explosives... and Bone-Flour to feed farm animals... oh yes! and Fertiliser to help him grow Victory Vegetables."
> "Gosh! I'll dig up *all* my old bones for salvage straight away." Bones—even gnawed ones—are vital to our war effort. If every family salvages only one bone weekly we shall free thousands of tons of shipping space for other essential needs. Save every scrap, even the smallest bones, and put out regularly for collection.
>
> *Remember* — Game, poultry and rabbit bones—though dangerous for dogs—are valuable salvage. Save them, too—besides all beef and mutton bones.
>
> This advertisement is contributed in the National Interest by the makers of **CHAPPIE DOG FOOD**

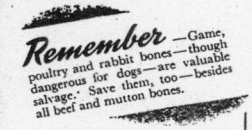

"At our place we go on working when the sirens go..."

Miss Margaret Bushell, has lived in Sarisbury nearly all her seventy years. To her, the war brought many restrictions. It meant that you couldn't go out when you pleased because there probably wouldn't be a bus to take you where you wanted to go.

Cycling was the only reliable means of getting from A to B – and it was on her bicycle that she experienced the D-Day operations.

"Anybody who is younger than I am wouldn't remember how we were geared to war. There was very little feeling of excitement, or disappointment or joy. Life was mostly work and bed. Even when we went out at weekends, we were unable to get any transport to go anywhere.

"If you tried to get the bus from Park Gate, all the people who had got on at Warsash completely filled it up, so unless somebody got off at Park Gate, you had no chance of getting on and you ended up going nowhere. There was no petrol and your bike was your only means of getting about.

"The troops arrival didn't change our lives, apart from very close on to D-Day when Warsash was shut off, roughly in the region of Greenaway Lane.

"I was working at Air Service Training, the aircraft factory, and I used to get the bus that went up Brook Lane every morning. On D-Day, I walked down the drive of Coldeast, where there had been tents either side and all was silent – there was nobody there at all. My mother said there had been an invasion so I hopped on my bike and cycled to Hamble where I took up my duties for the day.

"It was so quiet – there were no cars, no transport of any kind, the birds were singing, my bike wheels were humming and that was all you could hear. There was a feeling of everywhere being very, very deserted."

Miss Bushell, was used to seeing the troops, as they had been in the area since February of that year. She had become friendly with some of the soldiers stationed near her home and had invited several to her birthday party. But the celebrations did not turn out as she had planned.

"My 21st birthday was on May 25. I was to have had a party and I was very lucky, I had a beautiful birthday cake with spun sugar icing in white, pink and blue, made for me by the chef of a very prominent Hampshire family. But in the end there was no party because the troops had all been shut in behind the wire, so my mother and myself just sat and ate cake together."

———————————— ◆ ————————————

Mrs Olive Woolcock, from Stubbington, was in service at Southwick House until the Royal Navy requisitioned the house in order to create the Combined Allied Forces Headquarters.

Prior to the Navy taking over, Mrs Woolcock can remember stoking the fires, cleaning the carpets and polishing the furniture for the owner, Colonel Thomas Thistlethwaite. It was hard work but on the whole she enjoyed her years in service and remembers with fondness the tasks she had to perform.

"I was third house maid. I had to clean the gentry's rooms, like the library and the lounge. They had a huge drugget, which was a red carpet – just like they put down for the Queen – and that ran the length of the hallway. We had to put tea leaves down on the floor or wet paper and sweep it with a hard carpet brush. We had to clean the front by six thirty in

The Ovaltine Girl — **The Land Girl**

Both on National Service

THE importance of the care and cultivation of the land in the interests of the nation's food supply has been emphasized by wartime conditions. But for very many years some of the richest of Britain's farms and fields have been cultivated and used to produce the finest of those natural foods which constitute the ingredients of the nation's favourite food beverage—delicious 'Ovaltine.'

To-day, as always, the unrivalled resources of the famous 'Ovaltine' Farms and the 'Ovaltine' Factory in a Country Garden are producing in 'Ovaltine' a food beverage outstanding in quality and possessing the nutritive elements required to build up health, strength and vitality to the highest level.

Drink delicious **Ovaltine** and keep fit for Service

Use PEPSODENT – the IRIUM tooth paste

Toothpaste or Tooth Powder
7½d 1/3 and 2/2 (inclusive of tax)

IRIUM makes PEPSODENT give teeth healthy lustre

the morning, before Colonel Thistlethwaite came down. The first time I ever used a vacuum cleaner was at Southwick House. When we were polishing the furniture, it would take nearly all day because we had to move the furniture and use beeswax.

"The head house-maid was Barbara Poole. She would come round and run a finger over the furniture, to make sure we had cleaned it properly – so we couldn't get away with not dusting. The last job of the day was to make sure the Colonel's room was warm. He slept right at the top of the house in a four poster bed with steps at the side, which he used to get into the bed."

Mrs Woolcock received the princely sum of £2 a month for her labours – although her food and board was provided. Each member of staff was given half a pound of dairy butter a week – and if Mrs Woolcock had any spare, she would take it home to her mother.

On days off she would go into Portsmouth with her friends and she can still picture the destruction she saw there.

"One time when we went to Portsmouth, it must have been just after an air raid and I can remember seeing the strangest sight. Opposite the Theatre Royal, near the Guildhall, a house had been totally destroyed and all that

Southwick House – D-Day Headquarters

was left was a dresser with some cups on it. All the building was gone but the dresser was left with those cups on it and I just couldn't believe they had survived when everything else had gone."

If the maids went out with their boyfriends, they had to make sure they were back by 10 o'clock at night or face the wrath of Colonel Thislethwaite. And even if they made it back by the allotted hour, they still had to get past the sentry on the gate.

"The sentry on duty at the main gate would say `Stop, who goes there, friend or foe?' and we had to say `friend.' I was always very nervous and I would say `friend' as quickly as I could."

Mrs Woolcock can remember when the Royal Navy arrived to take over the house and she went with Colonel Thistlethwaite to his new home at Broomfield House. She also recalls how her boss took a while to adjust to his new surroundings. He seemed to miss Southwick and would often return to his former home.

"It broke the Colonel's heart. He went missing one day and he had made his way back to Southwick House to go to his wine cellar. It was very sad because that was his home and it took him a long time to settle down at Broomfield Park."

Her days of service came to an end when Mrs Woolcock realised she must enrol for war work. She heard of a job going at Percy M. See's boatyard in Fareham – and started in the boat building shop in about 1943.

"I can't remember what sort of boats they were that we worked on but I can remember using a clenching iron and `putting up' the nail holes. There were quite a few women working there.

"My friend and I made boiler suits out of black-out material. We bought a pattern and made them up at my friend's house. You couldn't buy anything like that because of rationing, so you had to make it yourself."

---------- ◆ ----------

Mrs Elizabeth Ward, was working in a munitions factory in Portchester when 6th June came. She went there when she left school and started off on the factory floor and progressed to the inspection department. She has lived in Portchester all her life and is well versed to talk about what life was like there, half a century ago.

"When I first left school I worked at Hayters, it was a garage that had been taken over for a munitions factory. I started on the factory floor and eventually went upstairs to the inspection department. We checked all the work with gauges, I wasn't very bright but I suppose they thought I was good enough."

While she was working at Hayters, Mrs Ward found a way of getting good value for her clothing coupons.

"Often we couldn't afford new clothes, so we would sell our clothing coupons to the Hayter girls and buy some of their old clothes because they used to have such nice things. Their clothes were much more expensive than we could have afforded but most of the time, we used to just make do with what we had."

Mrs Ward's father, Thomas Marchant, was head gardener at Murrells House in East Street, Portchester. He had Land Army girls to help him look after the bees and tend the flower beds. Mr Marchant was allowed to have his own allotment in the grounds for growing much needed vegetables for his family.

As well as working at Murrells, Mr Marchant was a volunteer fireman and when the call came, he would down tools and rush to fight the flames.

"I remember my father telling me about a fire at the piggeries along by where Smith's Crisps used to be in Southampton Road. It had been set alight by incendiary bombs and we could hear these poor pigs screaming. My father went to look in the shelter, to make sure the people living near there were alright and found it was full of pigs."

Land Army Girls at Murrells House

Portchester had a village atmosphere and was well served by its own shops. Mrs Ward recalled that one of the most popular places was the local sweetie shop.

"Mr Attrill's sweet shop was in West Street in Portchester. He used to make all his own sweets on the premises and you used to see him with a long piece of sugar stamping out the sweets. It was mostly boiled sweets that he made. The servicemen on leave used to use his shop a lot and I suppose they used to buy their cigarettes from him as well.

"My mother used to make mintoes from national dried milk because my Dad used to like to have some sweets and I suppose that helped out with our ration."

Portchester was by no means at the thick of it when it came to memorable wartime dramas. The local families had put to up with their fair share of ups and downs but life was by and large pretty uneventful. So, when a mysterious man was arrested on spying charges, Portchester became the centre of intrigue and speculation.

"My friend's mother was an invalid and one day a man came to the house. He told her there was a light showing from the house and asked if he could come in. He went through the house and out into the garden, which had the railway running at the end of it. She didn't think much of it, until later it emerged he was caught signalling to the planes, which were coming over because the Germans were trying to bomb the railway."

───────── ◆ ─────────

Mrs Connie Norton, from Park Gate, started working at Lankester and Crook, the grocers, when war broke out. Initially she had taken the place of her brother who had joined the services – but as the conflict progressed and the manager was called up for duty, Mrs Norton took charge of the Park Gate shop.

It was a difficult time due to rationing and Mrs Norton had to ensure that all her customers got their fair share. She had to deal with the bureaucracy that went with the coupon system of rationing.

"We only had supplies for our registered customers. If you were registered with Lankester and Crook's, you had to get your rationed goods there and you couldn't go anywhere else. We were supplied with enough food to cover the number of customers who

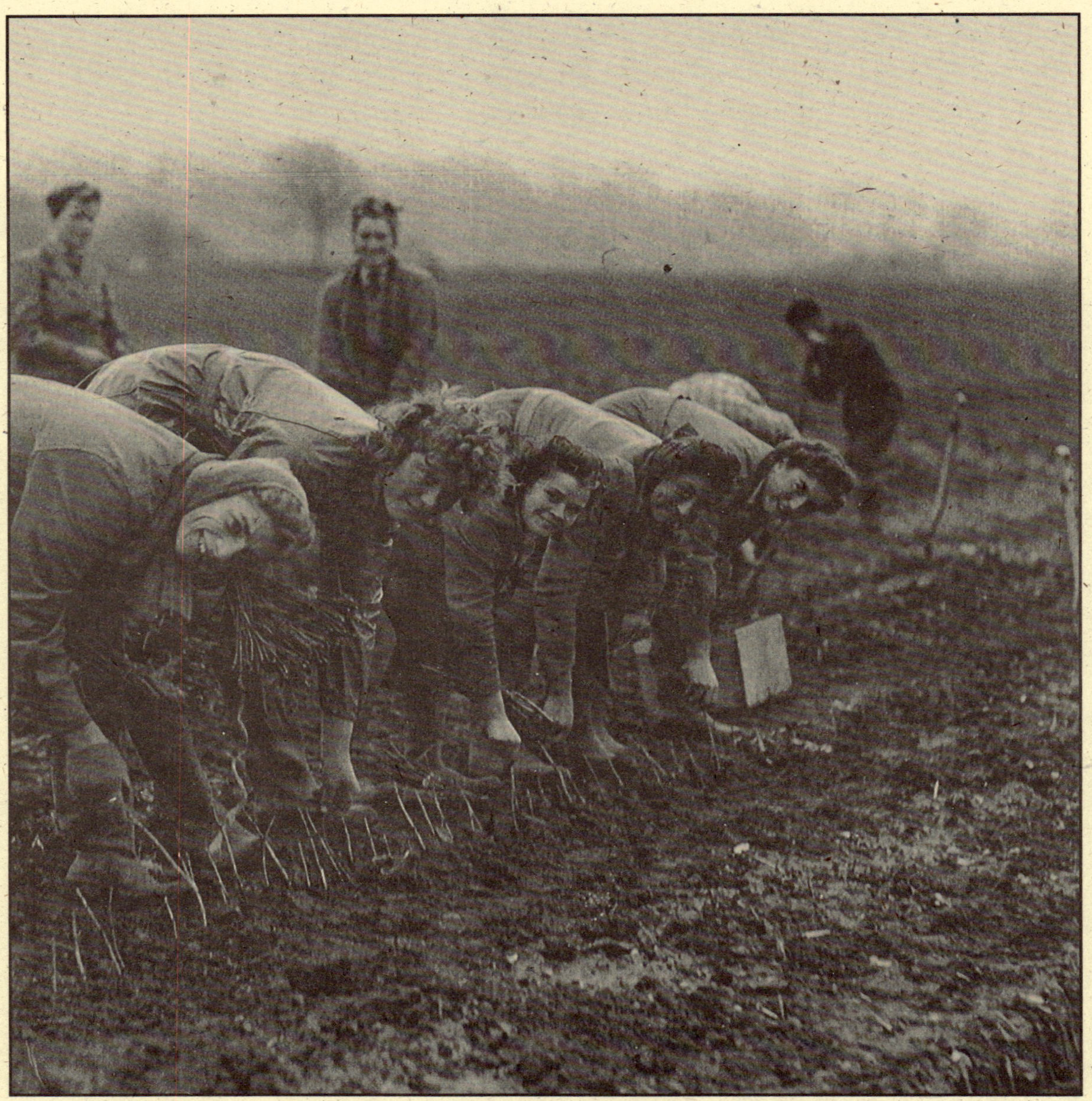

were registered with us. They brought their ration books in and we would cut the little tiny coupons out – they were like postage stamps. You had to be so careful because they all had to be counted up at the end of the week and they went to the Food Office in Fareham at Forrester's Hall.

"We were always weighing up because all the rationed items had to be put into little packages. You had 2oz of butter, 4oz of bacon, 4oz of sugar and 4oz of marg and lard.

"I used to have a side of bacon every week and that was all cut up into rashers. A whole cheese weighed 80lbs and we would get half of one of those or sometimes only a quarter but we had enough to supply our registered customers every week – we never let them down. A lot of things like custard powder, jelly and blancmange, were in short supply. We would get some of these things in our weekly order. We used to store it in deep drawers and when they were full up, I used to say that we could let every customer have something the same week.

"Some customers were very awkward but on the whole they were pretty good. We had one old lady, she came from Lower Swanwick on the five o' clock bus every night because she was working in the day. We used to close at five o' clock and so, being the manageress, I would serve her because all the shop girls had gone. She was a bit of a moaner because she had to work but she had to do her shopping some time."

As well as the day to day running of the shop, Mrs Norton had to ensure that fresh emergency supplies were also on hand in the event of a disaster.

"In one of our store rooms at Lankester and Crook's, we had some emergency supplies, which I was in charge of. I had to change them over every month and bring the supplies into the shop and replace them with fresh stuff, like margarine and butter. They were kept there in case of an emergency."

Mrs Norton, can recall taking on her managerial post with some trepidation but she quickly got to grips with the job and she was not frightened to fight for the rights of her staff.

"It was a very cold shop and we asked the Managing Director if we could have some heat – so he gave us a little oil stove – which was useless really. So then I asked him if we could wear slacks. It was unheard of then for girls to wear trousers but he gave us permission."

Baker, Mr Len Hobden, certainly learnt the meaning of hard work when he supplied bread for the Fareham area, from his bakehouse in Gosport Road.

"Work, work, work – everyone wanted bread. All my life consisted of, was between my house and the bakery. I worked 100 hours a week for three years without a break – not a Saturday or a Sunday off."

In addition to supplying the local people, Mr Hobden had contracts to supply Southwick and Fort Wallington. Whatever was going on in the outside world, the bread-making had to continue, to meet the never ending demand. Even when there were air-raids, the baking would continue regardless.

"With the machines, you couldn't hear the sirens but you could always tell when there was a raid on because you could hear the toilets flushing. I used to say there must be an air raid on – `Cos hark to all the lavatories going!' Even when we knew there was a raid on, we would carry on shooting out bread. We were selling it so fast we would have queues down Mill Road into Gosport Road.

"One of the worst things was the blackout – during the Winter, you were alright because you could keep cool. But in the Summer, when you had everything blacked out, the heat in that bakery was so terrific you could make your dough and watch it come up, you worked in just a pair of underpants and shoes – it was so hot."

The system of Bread Units, which was introduced to make sure there was enough bread to go round, was deemed unworkable by the bakers and Mr Hobden can remember that it was largely ignored.

"The public had books of Bread Units and they were entitled to so much bread a week but the Government had to give up the system because it never worked. If you had a family, say with six children, bread was all they had to live on and what baker was going to turn them down when they needed bread. In the end no baker tried to work with the Bread Units.

"What used to happen, was that people gave us their books and we made sure they had the right amount of bread. I mean what baker was going to carry a pair of scissors to cut out little coupons? All I used to do was cut up the Bread Units, bung them in a jiffy bag, then

I used to put a fictitious number down and they always used to pass it ... and we used to try to let people have just as much as they wanted."

The task of actually delivering the bread was also a bit of a headache, as petrol was in such short supply. Often they would trundle out to deliver the bread, only to discover their customers had been bombed out and been forced to move home.

"We did contracts for Southwick and Fort Wallington. Sometimes there wasn't a scrap of petrol to carry on our deliveries. Later on in the war, when they closed Fort Wallington, they put us over to Botley and I said they would have to come over and get it themselves. When they loaded up the lorry, they kicked all the bread up to the end – you had taken all that care and attention and they couldn't care less.

"We had our private deliveries as well as our contracts. We might go to Portchester, say, and if there had been a bomb, we would lose 40 to 50 clients just like that – we would never see them again."

With such a busy work schedule, Mr Hobden was grateful for all the helping hands he could get. So when a young man presented himself and offered to share the load, he was welcomed with open arms. However, this was one occasion when Mr Hobden should have checked out the teeth of this particular gift horse.

"I had an old man helping me, who was a dough-maker and there were women doing the rounds. One day, this young lad came up to me and said he had been invalided out of the Army, so I took him on. I'm a baker and I don't study insurance cards or that sort of thing. Anyway, one Sunday night he didn't turn up and to cut a long story short, it turned out he was a deserter. They found my van, minus the cash and eventually picked him up in Leeds. The court was held at the top of Stoke Road and when I gave evidence, the magistrates more or less blamed me for aiding and abetting."

──────────── ◆ ────────────

SIX

Soldiers were the best wartime playmates a child could wish for in Fareham. As the tanks and military vehicles of mainly American and Canadian troops rumbled into the borough for June 6, a very special time was about to unfold for countless children in Fareham and the surrounding area.

While mums and dads would often complain about their youngsters getting under their feet and making a mess, these new 'grown-up' chums on their doorstep had seemingly endless patience. They had time to talk and would allow their tanks to become the best adventure playground a child could imagine. Even if they couldn't be directly involved, the children just loved to watch as the men waterproofed their vehicles and made ready for the battle ahead.

American and Canadian troops, were particularly good to have as friends because they had something very special – CHOCOLATE.

After years of going without – and in some cases never knowing the joy of chocolate – suddenly here were these kind men with a seemingly endless supply of the stuff.

The war, by and large, had proved to be an exciting and adventurous time for children living in the Fareham area. While parents had a greater understanding of the full horror of battle, youngsters revelled in their new upside-down world.

Shrapnel, picked up by eagle-eyed youngsters on raids to bomb sites, was a treasured item and some boys and girls amassed huge collections.

They loved to watch the bombing raids that lit up the skies over Portsmouth and Southampton. Geographically, Fareham offered them the perfect vantage point and they thought little for their own safety. Even when the bombardment came closer to home and they could feel the rush of air on their skin that would follow the blast of a nearby bomb, they continued to find it all just a great adventure.

It seems that most parents had quite a time of it, when it came to persuading their children into the safe but most often damp shelter.

However, despite the fascination of the bombing raids, it was the arrival of hundreds of tanks on the roads outside these youngsters homes that was to bring the most excitement.

The friendships that grew between these troops and local children have stayed fresh in the mind even though they were formed half a century ago.

Mrs Christine Neville, from Bridgemary, can still remember the pride she felt as a four-year-old child being taken to school by a Canadian soldier, who had become friendly with her family.

"We lived with our grandmother at Beehive Cottages in Wickham Road, Fareham and the tanks were right outside our back door, on the Old Turnpike, for about eight weeks.

"They were mostly Canadians and each house adopted one of the tanks as their own. They used to wash in our house and use the place as somewhere to relax.

"There was one particular Canadian, called Bert Proudly, who used to take me to school in Osborn Road and I can remember feeling so proud as we walked together. He had a little girl of his own, called Melba and I think he liked me because I reminded him of his own daughter.

"There was a little cafe in Wickham Road, where the garage is now, and the Canadians used to take all us kids up there for breakfast. We had ham sandwiches and mugs of tea, I can still remember the sandwiches were more bread than filling – but we felt so grown up."

About three or four weeks before D-Day, military ambulances began to arrive and they were to offer a new source of delight for the youngsters. Mothers never had to search for long to find their children because they knew exactly where they would be.

"The ambulances were the other side of the Turnpike and the people with them were very kind to the children. They would let us go inside for our afternoon nap and then the mothers would come and get us later."

However, it was the tanks which really captured the childrens' imagination. They were the biggest and best toys the youngsters had ever dreamt of and they were right outside their houses, just waiting to be played with.

"We were all really good at climbing in and out of the tanks. There was one quite funny incident I will always remember. The Canadians and their tanks were having an inspection

Christine Neville in fancy dress

on this particular day. Everything was spit and polish because the Commander was coming round. "One little boy, who was about eight, asked if he could help. They gave him a tin of white paint to paint a particular part of the tank. He did that but then he got a bit bored and started to paint out all the insignia. He had done this to about eight tanks before anyone noticed what had happened. He was covered in paint, so the troops had to clean him up and get out the turps to clean up their tanks. I can remember the panic and thinking to myself – I don't know what all the fuss is about."

The kindness shown by the servicemen to Fareham families was equally reciprocated. They may not have had a lot to give but what the families had they gladly shared with their new found friends.

"There were always cups of tea for everyone and very often they were just troops who pulled in for a rest and then they pulled out again.

"One night at about 11 o'clock, when my Mum was just going to bed, she heard some lorries pull up outside. There were about half a dozen of them out there. She put her head out of the window and asked how long they were going to be there. They said they were just having a rest so she asked if they wanted some tea. She used the last of her tea and sugar ration to make them all a drink and opened up her last tin of meat to make them some sandwiches. She took it all out to them and told them to leave the cups and things on the doorstep when they had finished. The next morning, she went down and found they had left their rations of tea and sugar and anything else they had with them, on the doorstep.

"You always found that, during the war – you could give away your last bits of food but you would always get it back and often you would get back more than you had given. Everyone wanted to help. The general feeling was 'What I've got I'll share."

The troops were also good at getting hold of food for local families by using slightly unorthodox methods – but there were never any questions asked.

"Among the men outside our house was a Mexican fellow, who was typically how you would imagine a Mexican to be. He flirted with all the women, whether they were five or ninety-five years old and he was always singing and laughing. He was also well known for pinching things. He would go off at night and come back with a load of chickens. If anyone said they needed such and such a thing, he would come back with it. He would go off to the headquarters at Roche Court and come back with all sorts of stuff. He was so carefree and happy and he would keep everyone in fits of laughter."

As a little girl, Mrs Neville did not know the meaning of the word fear and she loved to watch the bombing raids with her mother, Madge Rogers. "I always wanted to go outside when the air raid was on, to watch the lights. My Mum never tried to stop me, she just took me out and held me in her arms.

"Directly opposite our cottage was an alleyway and on this particular night, when we were out watching, they must have been bombing Portsmouth and coming quite close by. Something went off directly in line with the alleyway and the blast hit us and my nightdress went up over my head and I can remember feeling so cross about it."

Air raid practice was a part of school life and children were used to leaving their classrooms at a moment's notice, to assemble in the shelters. The safety precautions were drummed into them, so they would know exactly what to do if the siren went off during school hours. They did not seem to mind the disruption and often it was a welcome diversion

TIME MARCHES ON...

AND SO, WHEN PEACE RETURNS, WILL

IDRIS
THE QUALITY SOFT DRINK

"Curiously enough, I'm Frederick Alan Potter, and this is my brother Sebastian Potter..."

from spelling and sums.

"There were two big shelters built in the playground. About three times a week, we had to have air raid practice. A whistle was blown and we had to march out at double quick time to the air raid shelter and stay there for about a quarter of an hour. I can only remember going into our family shelter once. It didn't have a door or wall in front of it. It was just a hole dug into the ground, with corrugated iron and earth on top of it."

When D-Day dawned and all the troops who had become so much a part of the Fareham community disappeared under cover of darkness – it was probably the children who felt it most. Many couldn't understand where they had gone or why they had left so suddenly – all they knew was that they had lost some of the best pals a child could possibly have.

"I can remember them not being there but I probably thought they were coming back. A few weeks before D-Day, they had come in during the evening and said they were off now, cheerio and thanks for everything. But about 24 hours later, they all came back, soaking wet and they never said a word about where they had been.

"I suppose I thought they would come back again, like before but then we heard the announcement on the radio and we knew they were really gone. It was a sad time and I missed them very much because they were so kind and such fun to be with.

"I had a persistent nightmare about Mr Proudly, when I was a child and it lasted for about six or seven years. It wasn't a nightmare that frightened me but I used to wake up feeling sad."

Ultimately, Mrs Neville remembers those formative years with great fondness and would not swap her childhood for the world.

"The war was a way of life for us. We were not old enough to be scared by it and we weren't old enough to understand. I was growing up and becoming aware of things around me. I had so many people to play with and we were encouraged to go and talk to the soldiers because nobody ever thought anything bad would happen.

"We were very happy children."

───────────── ◆ ─────────────

Mr Noel Coffin, lived in Trinity Street, Fareham and was 12 years old when the tanks and soldiers started to arrive for D-Day.

He can remember digging the family shelter with his father, at the onset of the war and seeing the big water tanks in Osborn Road that the fire brigade used. The black letters SWS (static water supply) can still be made out on the brick wall, where Osborn Road bends near the Drama Centre.

"I remember the dog fights in the skies over Fareham and we could always distinguish between the German and English aircraft.

"There was a Home Guard unit in Fareham and they were very nearly on the same lines as Dad's Army. We used to laugh at them but they were doing their bit.

"Nobody of my age can forget the turning point of the war, which was the build up of the allied forces ready for D-Day. Every street was just choc-a-bloc with army vehicles. They were parked all the way up Trinity Street.

"My mother and all her neighbours used to have fires blazing in the outhouse so that we had plenty of boiling hot water every day. The soldiers would come round and have a bath and the women would wash their clothes for them. They were one of the family and they were invited in, to join us for cups of tea. I used to stand and watch them putting mastic over all the electric components ready for the sea crossing.

"When the day finally arrived, the sky was black with aircraft. The whole sky from Titchfield to Portsdown Hill was absolutely full up.

"I wouldn't change my childhood for the world – it was the best."

———————— ◆ ————————

Mr Bob Mason, was living in Titchfield and had just turned 15 years old, as the build up to D-Day began in earnest.

"Virtually everybody in Titchfield had two or three Commandos that had been billeted with them. We had three living with us. They used to go off at night and come back in the morning – they used to tell us all sorts of stories. They were making commando raids over to the other side just before D-Day.

"One of them had a machine gun – a bren gun – and he would get down on the carpet, in front of the fire and take it all to bits. He used to let me have a go and I ended up being nearly as good as him.

"We used to have our milk delivered. They would come round from the farms with a big can of it and measure it out with a half pint gauge. When it had settled we used to skim the cream off the top and on Saturday nights, we would sit round the fire listening to Tommy Handley on the radio and take it in turns to shake this big jar with cream in it. Eventually, after shaking it for ages, the cream would turn into a little piece of butter.

"We were lucky because we used to keep rabbits and we would have stews and things like that. We used to get free cartridges to shoot them, so they didn't eat the crops. We used to help each other as well.

"If you had cabbages and somebody else didn't, you would do a swop with them. A lot of people used to grow their own vegetables. Everybody dug their gardens and nobody's garden was overgrown. They were all growing spuds – you had to or you wouldn't have anything to eat."

Like most young lads, Mr Mason enjoyed a game of football but it was unheard of for anyone to have a proper kit. You would turn up in whatever clothes you were wearing at the time and just get on with the game.

"There weren't even football boots. You either had old pairs of shoes, that you found or had been handed down to you – or you played in wellington boots and trousers. All your clothes were handed down. At the start of the war I was still wearing my brother's clothes and the sleeves were often too long. You had holes in the soles of your shoes and it was nothing to walk about with your toes poking out of your shoes."

Memories of the build-up to D-Day, are still fresh in the mind of Fareham councillor Mrs Ruth Godrich. As a 15 year-old schoolgirl, she can vividly remember the hundreds of Canadian troops camped on the recreation ground in Park Lane, where the leisure centre now stands.

During the months leading up to June 6, there was an air of expectation in and around Fareham. The massive influx of troops and top secret preparations at Stokes Bay transformed this small market town into a place of great military importance.

"As June 6 came, the Canadians were pretty well packed solid. They slept in tents and their vehicles. I remember walking up Park Lane and seeing all the vehicles parked on the grass verges. The men were covered in oil. They used to work on their vehicles all the time – they had to be ready because they didn't know when they were going."

Although everyone was living under the

Mrs Godrich's mother, Evelyn King (centre)

restrictions of rationing, Fareham people thought it only natural to share what little they had, with the ever growing ranks of allied soldiers.

Mrs Godrich's mother, Evelyn King, was a Wren at HMS Collingwood and was among those who felt sorry for the soldiers, whom she believed were not very well fed.

"I remember her coming home from Collingwood one day and saying `I'm going to do something for those boys.' So she baked some bread, picked some tomatoes from the garden and made them tomato sandwiches. She gave them to me and my sister Barbara to take down to the Canadians and they gave us bars of chocolate – which we thought were absolutely marvellous because we hadn't seen chocolate all the war."

Bill King, Mrs Godrich's father, had been seconded to help out in the hush-hush work at Stokes Bay because of his knowledge of marine craft. Bound by secrecy, he was not allowed to disclose the nature of his work – but he could not resist letting his young daughters know when a visiting VIP was expected.

"He kept very quiet about the work he was involved in but occasionally he would say to me... `If you or Barbara are anywhere near the top of Portland Street at about midday tomorrow you might see something interesting.' And along would come the police and some troops and Eisenhower, the King or Montgomery. Sometimes they were in open top vehicles and you would be just a few yards away from them.

"It's quite something years later to think `yes, I saw them.'"

When the historic day finally arrived, Mrs Godrich was in no doubt that the destiny of Europe lay in the hands of those brave young men.

"We knew that it was D-Day because when we woke up in the morning they were all gone. And we knew they were going over to try to move through France and end the war."

——————— ◆ ———————

School lessons were very restricted during this time because of the air raids that used to take place. In fact Mr Jim Murray, who was born in West Street, Fareham can recall that most of his lessons were nothing more than nature rambles – but he and his friends didn't mind.

These classes on the hoof took local children to beauty spots in the Meon Valley,

Portsdown Hill and the south of Fareham. Teachers felt safer taking these 'walks on the wild side,' rather than staying in the classroom under the constant threat of attack from the air.

The market town that Mr Murray and his friends regarded as home had changed dramatically in the months leading up to D-Day.

Mr Murray, a Fareham Borough Councillor, was able to cast his mind back fifty years to recall how the town used to be before thousands of troops arrived.

"It was a very compact place, the majority of shops were in the main street, with a couple of shops in Portland Street. It was a safe place to be, you didn't hear of things like crime and the local policemen were part of the family."

An abiding memory of how the town was to change in the run-up to the 'big-push,' was how the roads became heavily congested with army vehicles.

"They were crammed with tanks and other military vehicles. And where the golf course is now, there were lorries and trailers that used to put up the smoke screens."

These lorries were designed to belch out a thick, oily smoke to conceal the military build-up taking place on the streets of Fareham.

"Every night they used to come up through the town, towards the railway station, belching out filthy old oil – it was like a black rain cloud hanging over everything."

◆

Secrecy was the order of the day. A national poster campaign run during the war, warned everyone to keep 'Mum' as 'Careless Talk Cost Lives.' While preparations for D-Day were being made, it became imperative to keep the lid on the top secret plans and servicemen were ordered to be tight-lipped.

As a young girl growing up in Fareham, Miss Anne Ashton can remember how seriously everyone took the warning about wagging tongues. Her father was Mr George Ashton, the headmaster of Price's Grammar School and her family was naturally heavily involved in the life of the local community. But whereas nowadays military battles are media events, with round the clock news coverage, it was a very different story back in 1944.

"The whole atmosphere was one of being very careful. There were soldiers everywhere but they were very restricted in what they would say to civilians. My father had heard that King George V1 had inspected the troops and he tried to talk to them about it but they wouldn't even say a word about that."

As well as a running the school, Mr Ashton was an Air Raid Warden and memories of him in his uniform still make Miss Ashton chortle to this day.

"He would go out at night in his battle dress and tin helmet, looking exactly like the air raid warden in Dad's Army. When the air raid warning went at night, we used to use the underground cellar. Sometimes we slept down there all night and we would wake up in the morning feeling terribly dry because it was a bit airless down there."

As preparations for Operation Overlord gathered pace, many of the troops made their temporary home in the school grounds and the training room at the school was used for officers' meetings.

"I came back from boarding school and they were all there. They came and slept in the garden and they used the bathroom blocks for baths. And whenever I went out, my mother would say to me 'Mind you don't talk to any of the soldiers."

Dear Mr. Gerald :

I take up my pen in good time in order to send you Best Wishes on the occasion of your Birthday which should reach you five weeks from today. All at the Hall are well except old Mr. Macgregor who sustained a slight flesh wound near his asparagus beds by a bow and arrow discharged by a young evacuee. This evacuee is one of the ones stopping at the Lodge, and Mr. Macgregor had made him the bow and arrow himself, so he cannot complain. The silver is put away for the duration, but I take it out periodically and give it a careful clean. Last year we lifted a fine lot of potatoes from what used to be the Clock Golf Lawn. I am also looking after the cellar to the best of my ability. In particular, I have made a point of laying in a case of Rose's Lime Juice against your return. Like many good things, Rose's is hard to obtain in England these days. Still, there will be ample Rose's Lime Juice after the war, when all headaches and hangovers will be where they belong — on the other side of the Rhine.

In anticipation of that day, I sign myself, in haste.

Yours respectfully, Albert Hawkins
(Sergt., Home Guard).

There is no substitute for ROSE'S Lime Juice

One of Mrs Christina Merritt's most vivid wartime memories is of her evacuation from her home at Fleetlands, to the safety of the countryside. She was sent with her brothers and sisters to live with the Reverend Petter and she had never been away from home before.

"I was 10 years of age and it was the first time I had ever been on a train. We left from Gosport station and I can remember all the mothers waving to us. The train stopped in the middle of nowhere and we had to get out into a field. We were herded like cattle into this hut and people were there to choose which children they would take.

"We were three girls and a boy in my family and we were kept there until second to last and we thought that nobody wanted us. Then a woman dressed in a Red Cross uniform said she would take us. We got into her car and drove until we saw a great big house through the pouring rain. It was the vicarage at Durley and the Reverend Petter lived there.

Mrs Christina Merritt (far right) with her family

"We didn't even know where Durley was. We were going from a very poor family to someone who had maids and where you said prayers before every meal.

"When we arrived at the house, we went through the main door which was for the gentry and were told that was the last time we would use it – from then on we used the tradesman's entrance. We spent most our time with the maids.

"When we went to school, we had the `nit nurse' come to look at our heads. We had to have all our hair cut off and they said all the children from Gosport were lousy.

"I can remember on one occasion at Harvest Festival, the Vicar said I looked like a strong girl and gave me the heaviest pumpkin to carry to the church. The other children were calling things out at me, so instead of carrying the pumpkin I rolled it down the hill. It disintegrated and to teach me some discipline, the Vicar made me deliver the church magazine for a week. My brother had impetigo, a condition once known as the `kissing disease' and the Vicar wanted him to leave the house because it was so infectious. My Dad cycled all the way out to Durley to collect my brother and gave him a crossbar all the way home.

"We stayed a little bit longer but we were homesick – I can't remember if we stayed a year or six months but we went back right into the thick of it."

◆

Mr Roy Harvey

Mr Roy Harvey, from Locksheath, grew up in Brook bungalow in Brook Lane. He can still recall the terror he felt as an 11 year old child, with the build-up to D-Day happening all around him and constant air attacks overhead. But as well as the frightening aspects, there were some bonuses to growing up in the 1940s.

"There used to be a marquee where the Canadian troops held their film shows. If you went up Lockswood Road now, to where the mini-roundabout is, there is a house on the right hand side and that's where the marquee was.

"The films were in black and white, obviously and they were war films and we liked them, of course. I used to go there with my mates Ron Ayling, George Ayling and Peter Smith. The Canadians were a friendly lot and there was never any trouble."

While dramatic events are always easy to remember, it is often the small and seemingly unimportant details, which for some reason lodge themselves in the memory, ready to be recalled at a moment's notice.

"The thing that sticks in my mind and I know it sounds a bit silly, is that it was the first time I came across Bostik. In those days, they used it for sealing their vehicles up and I can remember getting some on my fingers and you couldn't get it off, it was just stuck on.

"When they were packing up to go for D-Day, the army asked my father if they could use the bungalow where we lived as a paying-out office. They would queue right round the front of the bungalow. They would come in the front door and get paid from a table they had set up in there. It used to go on all night and we were glad when it ended.

"It was a frightening time. As soon as the siren went off you would put your clothes on and go straight to the shelter. We were scared stiff a lot of the time."

──────────── ◆ ────────────

Wicor gang members, from Portchester, had no concept of fear as they dug out incendiary bombs from the mud flats near their homes. The teenage lads eagerly unscrewed the ends of the potentially lethal bombs, emptied out the phosphorous powder and proudly walked home with armfuls of the empty shell cases.

Looking back on this particular adventure 50 years on, Mr Ron Eacott, can still laugh at the naive daring of himself and his fellow gang members. He recalls the war years as a happy time but realises that he viewed the conflict with a child's mentality. As a grandfather now, he can appreciate the full enormity of the war and the price that many paid for peace.

But nothing can take away from the childish delight of watching dog fights in the skies above Portchester and having an enviable collection of shrapnel in his bedroom.

"I lived in Central Road, off White Hart Lane, in Portchester. We were called the Wicor gang because that was what this area was known as. There were about twelve or thirteen of us in the gang.

"One Saturday morning some planes came over and they dropped incendiary bombs, while the tide was out. They all stuck in the mud and you could see the fins poking out. We collected armfuls of them, screwed the bottoms off, took the powder out and kept them for souvenirs. We lit a bonfire with the phosphorous to get that nice blue glow – old Hitler didn't frighten us too much."

A good collection of shrapnel would inspire respect from your chums, in the same way that children today like to show off their collection of conkers or marbles.

Members of the Wicor gang would scour the streets looking for the mis-shapen bits of metal and debris that had fallen from the sky.

"After a heavy shelling from the forts, we used to go round the next morning looking for the biggest piece of shrapnel that we could find. We collected caps from shells and pieces of jagged steel – anything we could find."

Mr Eacott's father worked at HMS Collingwood and his mother was a cook at a local roadside cafe frequented by servicemen. By night, they became local fire watchers, using the stirrup pump, a bucket for water and another for sand, that they had been given. Every time the siren went off they had to be ready to run to the nearest fire.

Mr Eacott had his own important role to play as an ARP runner.

Mr Ron Eacott

"The thing that I can remember most is my work as an ARP runner. I was thirteen when I started, you were supposed to be fourteen but we lied when it suited us.

"There were two of us runners and as soon as the siren went off, whatever time of the night, we used to run to the ARP Warden's house in Nelson Avenue. By then the bombs would be dropping and the guns rattling and we used to run in and shelter under his table, where he had a Morrison shelter, which was a wire cage, like a pig pen.

"When a house caught on fire and they couldn't put it out with the stirrup pumps, it was my job to go from the ARP Warden's house and run to the fire station and bring a fire engine back to the nearest fire hydrant, to put the fire out.

"All the Portchester firemen had moved into Portsmouth and they had brought in firemen from Wickham and Alton and they didn't know the names of the roads in Portchester – so that was why they needed our help.

"One night I was sent down to get a fire engine from Portchester cross roads and while I was there a whole stick of bombs dropped on the A27. I got on the fire engine and we got back to where the bombs had dropped. The gas main was alight and the houses were all blown down. I had to come back to the ARP Warden, with a message from the fire brigade, that we would have to put our own fire out with the stirrup pump because they were too busy with bombs on the A27.

"I was a runner throughout the war, we weren't worried a bit, it didn't bother us at all."

There were barrage balloons near Mr Eacott's home and he can remember how the German pilots would shoot at them and they would explode before his very eyes.

"They used to come over on Sunday mornings and shoot all the barrage balloons. We used to watch them coming down on fire and then see who could find the biggest bit of balloon. It was a grey material and good for making bags and head scarves. When they replaced the barrage balloons, they would walk them from Titchfield along the A27, semi-blown up, holding them by the cables. There was one at the little school in Cranleigh Road and one at Cornaway Lane."

In 1943, aged fourteen, Mr Eacott left school and began work as a butcher's apprentice.

"I didn't have any choice. I was already working as a Saturday boy at Brudenells, the butchers in White Hart Lane. You got one and nine pence worth of meat but there were a few little fiddles going on – the ones that had the money, got the goods.

"I started at seven in the morning until seven at night. I used to have to scrub the shop down. Most of the beef was Argentinian. It would arrive in a great big frozen block and all the bones had been taken out. You had to hang it up for three days for it to thaw out."

BOVRIL
The 'Home' Guard

♦

Mrs Ruth Mould, lived in Portchester throughout the war. Her home was in Southampton Road, in the shadow of the landmark chalk pits. As a schoolgirl, she can recall the special place where the family would shelter, during the bombing raids that lit up the sky.

"A few of us had caves built, up in the chalk pit and I used to think we were going to be the only survivors left, when the bombs were really bad. The caves were drilled into the chalk and we drove to the chalk pit, when there was a raid on. We had beds in the cave, so we could sleep there and there was a primus stove and we used hurricane lamps, I remember. There were wooden doors on the cave so it could be locked up when we left.

"After a while, the radar station people came and made a place behind our caves. They drilled it out and put the radar equipment there. There were servicemen on guard then and one day they invited us in, to show us what they had done. From then, we had to have a pass to go up there."

By 1944 and the build-up to D-Day, Mrs Mould was a seventeen year-old working as a secretary for her solicitor father. The fear of the early years of the war was replaced with a fascination for the American and Canadian troops she met at the local dances.

"I used to go to tea dances, which ran from 4 o'clock to 6 o'clock in the afternoon and then I went to the ones in the evening as well and they finished at 10 o'clock. The tea dance cost one shilling and sixpence and that included the tea and a sandwich. There were tables and chairs set out and the troops came and they were served tea, a sandwich and cake. The band played and the soldiers came and asked you to dance and when you had finished, you went and sat down, finished your tea and then somebody else would probably ask you to dance.

"When the tea dance finished at 6 o'clock, there was a break and then the evening dance would start. The Americans didn't come to our tea dances so much. They had their own but they didn't sit round and have tea."

Dancing was Mrs Mould's passion and the relatively inexpensive pastime helped her to forget the war for a few hours, as she was swept around the dance floor.

"I was very keen on dancing and had lessons. I passed my ballroom exams in bronze, silver, gold and gold star. At this time you couldn't travel out of the county and that

Ruth Mould with Leo Gaume

caused some problems with my dancing exams. I was allowed to travel to London but I couldn't go along the coast, so when I had an exam in Hove, Sussex, I had to apply for a pass because otherwise you wouldn't have been allowed on or off the train."

The arrival of the servicemen brought great excitement and in common with many young girls of her age, Mrs Mould began dating some of the soldiers. To this day she has photographs of two special boyfriends, a Canadian, Jack Dyer, and an American, Leo Gaume.

"There were hardly any English soldiers here, we were completely taken over by Americans and Canadians. Southwick House at the back of the hill is where it was all going on, of course. A Canadian boyfriend of mine was in the woods on the other side of the hill. Those woods were all camouflaged with nets because the troops were there under canvas, waiting. I had a bike at this time and I can remember pushing it up the hill and cycling down the other side, where I was stopped by a policeman because `Monty' was coming along the road. He had a very distinctive black car.

"The Americans took over Hilsea completely and being Americans, they had their own dances, with bands brought in specially and they had their own Coca-Cola parlours. They brought some beautiful bands down and some of them were really quite well known. And the food they had, compared to us was amazing.

They used to bring my mother all sorts of food and chocolate of course.

"I liked all the Glenn Miller music very much and Frank Sinatra was the craze at that time. I remember when `In The Mood' came out, my father said it was just a lot of old noise and we would grow out of it."

Canadian sweetheart Jack Dyer

All these years on, Mrs Mould still has a special memory of the role her father's pigeons played in the build-up to D-Day.

"My father had racing pigeons and they had to join the RAF. He was a great pigeon fancier and to get the corn for them, he had to offer them for the RAF to use. They would come and get them from home and take them in the aircraft with them. If they saw anything unusual up there, they would send the pigeons back with messages.

"And I believe when they threw them out of the planes at such a speed, a lot of them broke their wings. So they put them in brown paper bags. I think the idea was that the bag would break first and give the pigeons more of a chance because they would be further away from the aircraft. When the Americans came, they took over the pigeons but they had to have a fellow in the garden all the time, with a jeep down the drive, waiting for them to come back. They had someone in our garden for a long time waiting for these messages to come in with the pigeons."

When June 6 arrived the area around Mrs Mould's home was a hive of activity, both in the air and on the ground. The friends that she had made went off to do their bit and her two boyfriends, from the time, let her know that they had survived the invasion.

"When the Americans were getting ready to go over, not the fighting ones but the ones who went after them, they used to take their ties away from them so they couldn't leave their camp. If they were seen out by the Military Police and they weren't wearing their ties then they knew they shouldn't be out at all. A lot of the troops were wearing the 'green flash' and I understand those were the ones that went over with the first wave.

"On D-Day itself, there was a roar of planes as they went overhead and on the A27, all the tanks and lorries were going one way – and within a short space of time, the ambulances were coming back the other way, taking the troops to hospital.

"After the invasion I did hear from the American and Canadian chaps I knew. The Canadian fellow, Jack, came back on leave and when he went back again, I think he was repatriated to Canada – so that was that. And I had lots of letters from the American, Leo, but he never got leave to come back and he was repatriated."

Mr Allan Cooper, who now lives in Wimborne St Giles, put his memories into words in a very special letter written for the project. He captured the mood of growing up in the Sarisbury Green and Brooklands Park area so well, that it was decided to reproduce his letter in its entirety.

"D-Day preparations were the most momentous time of my life. The big transit camp surrounded my home, it was set up by men of the Pioneer Corps. Hessian screened bucket lavatory cubicles, tin roofed, sprouted all over the camp. Some formed part of an ablutions block near our front hedge.

"A latrines notice was a grim warning until Captain Martin RN, one of our neighbours, had them moved up the Green by his wall, where daily emptying by hand over the barbed wire into a tanker might be less offensive.

"A tannoy in the cherry tree was another nuisance to BBC's Mr Vittoria, who was billeted with us. He had to sleep during the day. He sped home to the New Forest on days off. The loud speaker crackled endlessly; `So and so come at once to the Camp Commandant's office. Over and out'.

"Duckboard tracks separated lines of hundreds of tents. Road verges were bulldozed and hard shoulders laid. French Canadians scaled the wire with duck boards and mattresses to run away to the river and woods with village `maidens.' Columns of tanks, lorries and jeeps, moved in with masses of men including Irish Hussars, Canadian 3rd Anti-Tank Regiment and the Fife and Forfar Yeomanry (whose badges I have lost).

"Marquees were set up in Brooklands, for dining and concerts. Jessie Matthews was one of the visiting entertainers. I talked to her in old age in Dorset. She seemed lonely and went to live at Hatch End near London.

"Most weeks I and other boys were smuggled under the wire and canvas by soldiers. One evening when `leggy' Southampton dancers were to appear, a Camp Sergeant spotted us. `Wot the `ell's them kids doin' in `ere? He turned to soldiers by us and said... `There's a bloody war on. Someone spoke up for me.

`This one's Dad was killed in the Arctic, his house is practically on the Camp.' `Oh well then, keep yer bleedin' `eads down till the C.O.s sat down.

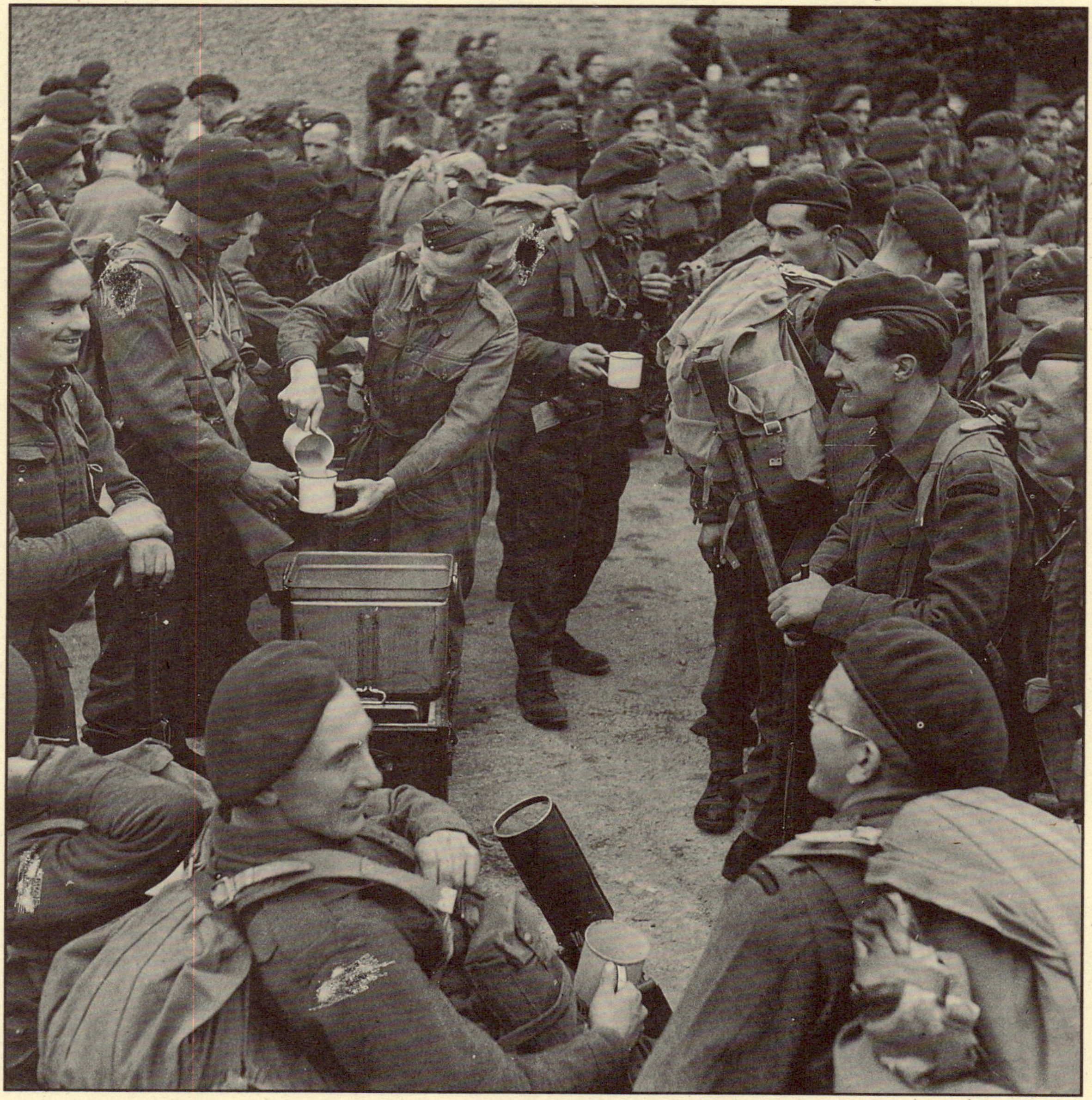

"There's no one kinder to children than the British Tommy. They rewarded us with eatables, when we cleaned their boots or begged our mothers to sew flashes on new uniforms. Powder needed to be shaken out of them. Keating's perhaps or anti-poisonous gas? We wondered. I watched the strenuous replacement of rubber sheathed tank tracks for all-steel battle tracks. Thick waste timber from packing cases helped me make a superb kennel for dog, Pat. He had just got used to it when he was abducted in a Canadian tank. Botley police found the lively pet and brought him home rejoicing.

"I, too, was given a ride in a Sherman tank, quite deafening. The squadron came to a halt opposite the main entrance to Cold East Hospital. `Jump boy, jump, heaven knows where we are going.'

"Just then a funeral cortege approached from the Green. I knew that it was the aunt of my neighbour, Tom Wallace. Moving as one man, the Canadians snapped to attention and saluted the coffin of a dear old lady who was being taken to Titchfield for burial.

"After pressure from me, my mother gave up her embossed Indian tin biscuit box, so that a soldier could carry his little treasures safely to Normandy. We chalked anti-Hitler slogans on the tanks.

"One morning I woke up in the dark and heard Infantry battalions marching away loudly singing `Paper Doll' and a sexy version of `Roll Me Over.' I blushed in bed wondering whether my mother was listening. I took seriously my dead Royal Naval father's command to `look after Mummy while I'm away.'

"Those uncountable warriors sounded so brave in their mass. In 1965, I walked between the lines of their headstones where many of them lay in Bayeux Military Cemetery: all so neat and quiet, valiant givers of their lives for our liberty."

——————— ◆ ———————

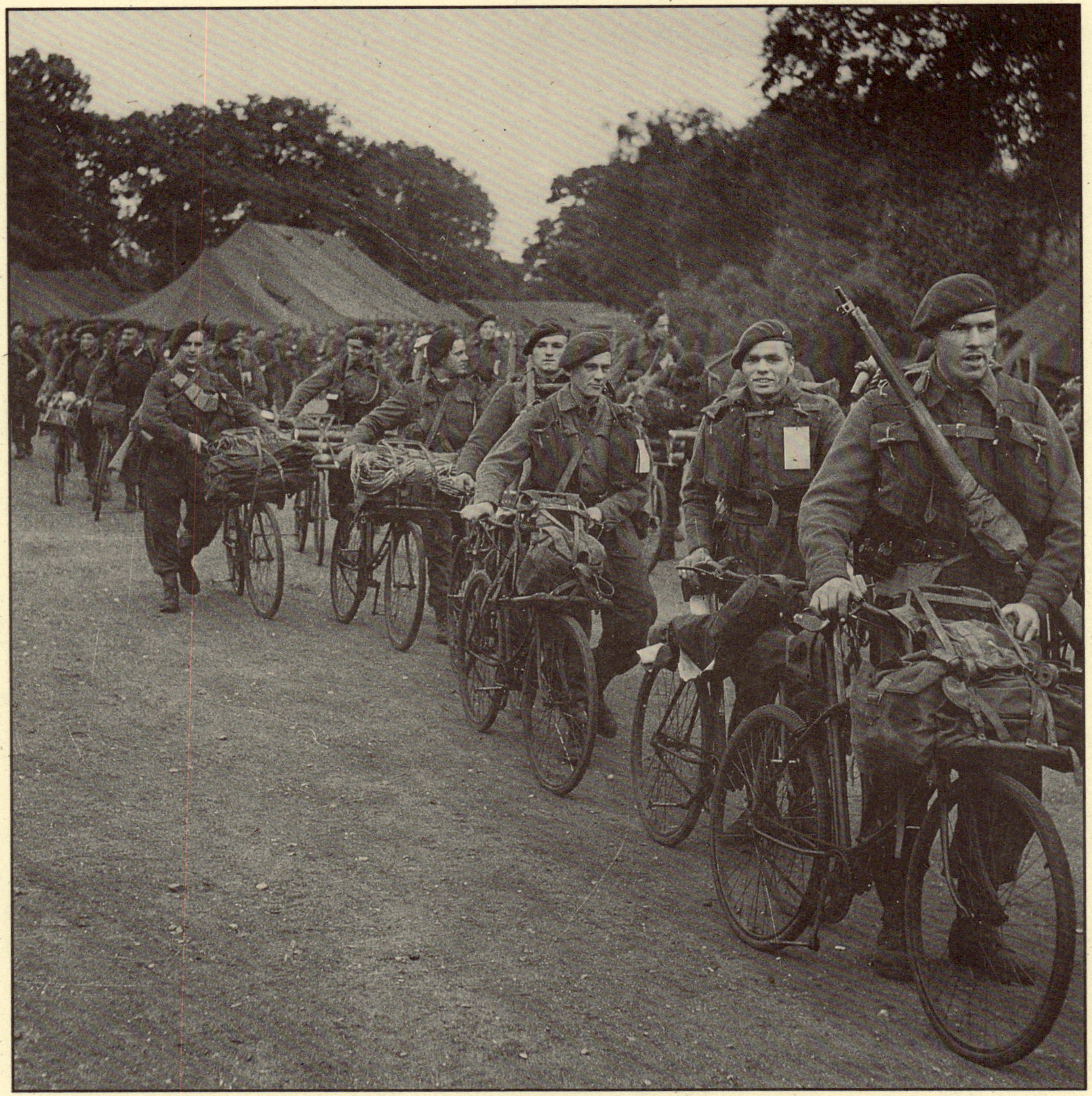

DESTINATION UNKNOWN

It had all seemed such fun!
One day the Canadians came,
parking their huge lorries
bonnet to tail along the road.
The young men, fit and strong,
settled easily to a gypsy life
in their camouflaged vehicles.
Sitting on the broad grass verges
they talked to everyone who passed:
winking and whistling at the girls,
offering gifts of chocolate –
they appeared happy and carefree.
Then one morning they had gone...
quietly and without trace.
They never came back!!!

Joan Miles Lister, Southsea 1994.

Joan Lister lived in Fareham until 1940, when her family was evacuated to Farnham.
She returned to Fareham in 1943 and worked
in the Holy Trinity Vicarage, while waiting to start training in children's work.

ACKNOWLEDGEMENTS

The Publishers wish to express their gratitude to the following people who kindly contributed personal accounts and photographs for this book.
Where possible maiden names have been included and are shown in brackets.

Mr Roy Fay
Mr Jim Morice
Mr Allan Davis
Mr Gordon Murphy
Mrs Diane Barnato-Walker
Mrs Gladys Andrews
Mr Joyce Kingswell
Mrs Rita Briggs (Goodson)
Mrs Patricia Macdonald (Ogden)
Mr Harold Holdaway
Mr Ken Riley
Reverend Ted Royds-Jones
Mr Pat Hamblin
Mrs Rhona Moody (Cleverley)
Miss Edith Strebor
Mrs Joyce Vare (Barnes)
Mrs Phyl Manuel (Marsh)
Mrs Freda Triggs (Stone)
Mrs Olly Pepperell (Hubbard)
Mrs Joan Collins (Newbury)
Mrs Lou Webb (Lockyer)
Mrs Winifred Bynam (Durrant)

Mrs Doris Cox (Butcher)
Mrs Margaret Beckett (Sheppard)
Mr Vernon Lees
Mr Dick Marshall
Mr Claude Daish
Miss Margaret Bushell
Mrs Olive Woolcock
Mrs Elizabeth Ward (Marchant)
Mrs Connie Norton (Colverson)
Mr Len Hobden
Mrs Christine Neville (Rogers)
Mr Noel Coffin
Mr Bob Mason
Mrs Ruth Godrich (King)
Mr Jim Murray
Miss Anne Ashton
Mrs Christina Merritt (Sparshott)
Mr Ron Harvey
Mr Ron Eacott
Mrs Ruth Mould (Hiley-Jones)
Mr Allan Cooper
Mrs Joan Lister

Additional photographs have been supplied by the following:

Imperial War Museum
H. M. S. Collingwood
H. M. S. Dryad

The News, Portsmouth
Mr Larry Walder
Mrs Margaret Jerrard

Special thanks to the D-Day team:- Bob Parkinson, Donald Hyslop, Kirsten Lanchester, Rob Townsend and all the volunteer interviewers.

120